PRAYING FOR
TEEN
BOYS

Also by Brooke McGlothlin

Praying for Boys

How to Control Your Emotions, So They Don't Control You

Hope for the Weary Mom Devotional
(cowritten with Stacey Thacker)

Gospel-Centered Mom

Praying Mom

Unraveled
(cowritten with Stacey Thacker)

Everyday Prayers for Peace

Everyday Prayers for Patience

PRAYING FOR
TEEN
BOYS

PARTNER WITH GOD FOR THE
HEART OF YOUR SON

BROOKE McGLOTHLIN

BETHANYHOUSE

a division of Baker Publishing Group
Minneapolis, Minnesota

Published by Bethany House Publishers
Minneapolis, Minnesota
BethanyHouse.com

Bethany House Publishers is a division of
Baker Publishing Group, Grand Rapids, Michigan

Printed in the United States of America

Library of Congress Cataloging-in-Publication Data
Names: McGlothlin, Brooke, author.
Title: Praying for teen boys : partner with God for the heart of your son / Brooke
   McGlothlin.
Description: Minneapolis, Minnesota : Bethany House Publishers, a division of
   Baker Publishing Group, [2025] | Includes bibliographical references.
Identifiers: LCCN 2024041945 | ISBN 9780764243721 (paper) | ISBN 9780764244643
   (casebound) | ISBN 9781493449682 (ebook)
Subjects: LCSH: Teenage boys—Conduct of life. | Teenage boys—Religious life.
Classification: LCC BJ1671 .M64 2025 | DDC 248.8/32—dc23/eng/20241115
LC record available at https://lccn.loc.gov/2024041945

Unless otherwise indicated, Scripture quotations are from the Christian Standard Bible®, copyright © 2017 by Holman Bible Publishers. Used by permission. Christian Standard Bible® and CSB® are federally registered trademarks of Holman Bible Publishers.

Scripture quotations labeled ESV are from The Holy Bible, English Standard Version® (ESV®), copyright © 2001 by Crossway, a publishing ministry of Good News Publishers. Used by permission. All rights reserved. ESV Text Edition: 2016

Scripture quotations labeled KJV are from the King James Version of the Bible.

Scripture quotations labeled *The Message* are from *The Message*, copyright © 1993, 2002, 2018 by Eugene H. Peterson. Used by permission of NavPress. All rights reserved. Represented by Tyndale House Publishers.

Scripture quotations labeled NKJV are from the New King James Version®. Copyright © 1982 by Thomas Nelson. Used by permission. All rights reserved.

Cover design by Micah Kandros Design

Baker Publishing Group publications use paper produced from sustainable forestry practices and postconsumer waste whenever possible.

25 26 27 28 29 30 31   7 6 5 4 3 2 1

To my sons, Max and Sam.

I haven't been a perfect mom. You know better than anyone just how many mistakes I've made. I don't look back on my motherhood and pump my fists in victory over my amazing parenting. But I do raise my hands in praise to the God who taught me to pray for you. There has never been a day of your life when your mom hasn't covered you with her prayers. It's the one thing I can say, with absolute confidence, that I got right throughout your lives, because to pray means to put all of my confidence in the God who made you and not in my parenting skill. Anything good that may come of being a part of our family comes directly from His work in your life, in spite of my imperfections. If my fervent prayers have partnered with God's plan for you, I will call this parenting thing a success.

Max, you are my favorite Max.
Sam, you are my favorite Sam.
Rise, and shine, and give God the glory.

CONTENTS

Foreword

I began writing online when my first two (of four) sons were young teenagers. As I shared blog posts about the trials and triumphs of raising boys, I was blessed with an invitation to join the writing team at the MOB (Mother of Boys) Society, led by Brooke McGlothlin and Erin Mohring (now Million Praying Moms). Though I was one of the older (or as I prefer to say, more seasoned) women on the team, I found great joy and wisdom in learning from other #boymoms in the trenches.

One of the most profound influences during this time was Brooke McGlothlin's first book, *Praying for Boys*. It taught me to pray with purpose and precision, using Scripture to address my growing sons' unique needs. I was learning that the teenage years are filled with growth, discovery, and challenges—moments that call for intentional prayer. Brooke's words encouraged me to fight for my boys (in prayer) rather than against them. This season sparked a deep passion in me for praying God's Word over my family.

Although Brooke was a younger mom, her wisdom—clearly God-given—mentored me in powerful ways.

Today, those two oldest boys are now young men, ages twenty-five and twenty-three, who live thousands of miles away from home. As they've grown, so have my prayers for them. (Parenting may change, but the importance of praying for our children never ends!) One of the greatest blessings of these years of prayer has been witnessing God's faithfulness. Reflecting on answered prayers fills me with gratitude and gives me confidence to keep praying, trusting God with everything ahead!

Today I am thrilled that more than a decade after her first book, Brooke is releasing *Praying for Teen Boys*. This is a book brimming with wisdom from her journey as a now seasoned boy mom. This resource is a true treasure.

Praying for Teen Boys is a prayer guidebook and a lifeline for anyone seeking to impact the life of a young man. In it you'll find Scripture-based prayers as well as practical insights into the unique challenges and triumphs teen boys face today. Each prayer aligns our hearts with God's purpose for the boys we love, equipping us to guide and encourage them as we bring them before their heavenly Father.

Through this book, Brooke equips us to approach prayer with confidence, knowing it not only shapes the lives of our sons but also deepens our own faith and reliance on God.

If I could make this book required reading for all parents of teen boys, I would! I imagine it will live by your bedside or be carried in your purse as you turn to it repeatedly. I encourage you to take full advantage of the mentorship and guidance found in its pages. And discover the blessing of praying God's Word, which He has promised will not return void.

—Monica Swanson, podcaster, author of *Boy Mom, Raising Amazing*, and *Becoming Homeschoolers*. Find her online at MonicaSwanson.com.

THE POWER OF FIGHTING <u>FOR</u> INSTEAD OF AGAINST

My older son, almost eighteen years old, is getting ready to head out the door for baseball practice. It's late in the day, and he's freshly showered, because they didn't have school today. I hug him, noticing that my head is resting solidly on his chest, and that his long, shaggy hair is still damp. He smells like his dad's cologne, and his truck keys are hanging out of the pocket of his shorts. I squeeze him hard, and he wraps his arms around me, picking me up off my feet to hug me and twirl me around the kitchen. He's stronger than he realizes, so his hug makes me squeak, and that makes us both laugh out loud. And it's in that moment that it happens.

He crinkles up his nose as he laughs.

Instantly, I'm transported from looking at my almost-adult's face to my little boy of just four years old. It's as if that younger, softer face is somehow transposed upon the older, more chiseled replica, and for just a moment I see my baby boy, chubby hand held out to his mama with a flower he'd picked just for her, and his blanket tied around his neck like a cape. My hero.

My heart squeezes, and it feels like the inside match to the hug I just got from the one who made me a mama. There will never, ever, be another him. My firstborn. My beautiful blond boy with freckles on his nose (that get worse . . . or better . . . in the sun), a gorgeous smile, and a heart that is growing up as big as his body.

I'm not sure if this phenomenon happens to all mothers, but I suspect it does. They seem to understand when I ask if they've ever seen an expression on their older son and instantly recognized their younger son in his place. When this happens, it squeezes my heart in a painful way, but it also serves as a reminder to me that I have a significant place of privilege in this young man's life.

There will come a day when I may not be the most important woman in his life, and that's okay. If God gives my son (either of them) the privilege of marriage, his wife will one day lead his heart, and he will lead hers. They'll build a family together, a life, and hopefully, serve God's kingdom with their time and talents, but no other woman on the face of the planet will be able to experience what I do.

I'm the only woman who will ever look at his face as a man and see the boy he once was. I'm the only woman who will have firsthand experience of what he had to fight through to get to where he is now. The only woman who watched him battle for what he wanted in his early life. The only woman who taught him to read, tie his shoes, and look for God's beauty all around him in this world. The only woman who held on so tight, only to have to forcibly let go . . . because that was my job.

The love young boys shower on their moms is often precious and full of sweetness. We are the first person with whom they want to share their world, their secrets, their hopes and dreams, and even their challenges. They defend us, adore us, and can't imagine their lives without us. But as they get older and the process of differentiation begins, moms are often left feeling the void of that precious, close relationship we once had. Sweet conversations are often replaced with arguments. Feeling "in the know" is trumped by feeling "in the dark," and the relationship that was once so strong now sometimes leaves us feeling like we and our sons aren't even on the same team.

One thing I know about having children who are out on their own, or are about to be, is that the way we parent changes, and that brings with it all kinds of emotions . . . good and bad. Gone are the days when we can control every little thing that comes into their lives. Gone are the days of being able to hold them close, or even being the most important person in their lives. And gone are the days when we have the right to make good decisions for them.

The teenage years are an emotional roller coaster and can bring with them many opportunities for sin, negative friendship experiences, and challenges to our efforts to help our sons choose to follow God and to see the world through the lens of His Word. Boys face temptations today that their parents never had to face, at least not in the same way, and this can cause some parents to shut down and take a hands-off approach, feeling a sense of loss and lack of purpose.

Yes, things change. But while our role might have changed, our purpose has not. Not if we know what our real in-Christ purpose is as a mom.

What if there was a way to learn to fight *for* our sons instead of *against* them? What if there was a way to partner with God for the hearts of our sons that has nothing to do with managing them, correcting them, or trying to force them into a mold of our making, but instead releases them to the good plans of their sovereign God, all the while helping Mom learn to walk in her constantly changing role with peace?

What if we could find the wisdom we need each day to help our sons through the challenging teenage years, and feel purposeful instead of powerless in our motherhood plan?

What if we could take joy in knowing our God-given role, releasing the rest to the God who holds it all together?

What if we could feel empowered by our ability to go to God's Word, because it has the power to change our son's heart and we trust it to do exactly what God purposes for him?

What if we could release our need to control, and choose to protect with our prayers instead?

What if we could have peace, knowing there will always be limits to what we can do, but there will never be limits to what we can pray?

Could there be a way for us to unlock the power of the prayer partnership God offers in our parenting so we can act with confidence on a regular basis?

This is the power of fighting *for* our sons in prayer.

I've seen it work in my own home as I've chosen to be a praying mom these last eighteen years or so. Not that it's perfect here; please don't think that. I'm an imperfect mom, with an imperfect husband and imperfect sons, and we all need Jesus. But isn't that just the point?

Maybe it's because I truly believe God will use everything in their lives—good, bad, or ugly—to lead them on the path He has for them, and that that path will look different from what I might've chosen for them. I believe this because I see it in my own life, and I see it on the pages of Scripture. And it's this desperate need for Jesus—to show me things I wouldn't see without Him, give me wisdom, hold everything together, give me peace, empower me through His Word, help me let go of control, and act with confidence—that gives me the purpose I need in this season, just as it will in the next.

Join me as we learn to give all of this to God in prayer, fighting *for* our sons instead of *against* them. The time is now to partner with God in prayer for the hearts of our sons.

How to Fight in Prayer

So how do we fight for our children in prayer? I think we first have to understand what prayer is and is not.

The simplest, most basic definition of prayer is conversation with God. Tim Keller calls it a conversation with God that He started.[1] In other words, God has invited each of us into a holy and divine partnership, where we share our hearts, fears, worries, confusion, and requests, and He gives us His wisdom, comfort, truth, love, and guidance in return. It isn't necessarily a fair partnership. He is still God and therefore has the right to tell us yes, no, or wait (and He will say each of these things at some point), but we get the most out of it by far. To think that we have the God of the Universe, who *created* the hearts of our sons, opening His arms in invitation to us, saying, "Seek wisdom here!" is powerful, and I don't want us to miss it. What mother wouldn't want to join in this kind of conversation to help meet the specific needs of her individual children?*

When I first came to prayer, it was because I was in desperate need for God to move in my home. I started praying because I wanted Him to change my children. I don't know if I would've admitted it then, but I think I believed that because prayer was a holy work, God would be obligated to answer mine the way I wanted Him to. Combine that with the fact that I was praying Scripture—God's Word itself—and I felt even more holy . . . like my prayers were a shoo-in. And in a sense, they were. God

---

* It isn't always easy to answer the question "Why in the world would we choose not to take advantage of the offer God gives us to ask Him for what we need most?" If you believe you should be praying but struggle with questions, feel too busy, don't know how or what to pray, or aren't sure your prayers really matter to God, I'd like to recommend pausing for a bit to read my book *Praying Mom: Making Prayer the First and Best Response to Motherhood*. It explores seven of the most common reasons moms struggle to have a vibrant prayer life and will provide you with the biblical perspective you need to take the next step.

will always cause His Word to have the exact effect He wants it to in a human heart (Isaiah 55:11).

It is true that praying God's Word will produce a specific outcome, but it is untrue that the outcome will be exactly what *we* want it to be or happen when *we* want. Many Christians believe prayer should work like a vending machine, where they put a request in and God spits the "right" answer out. But this is not so. God invites us to pray but retains the right to be God. We must never try to use prayer as a method of getting God to do what we want. Even praying His Word can be done with wrong motives, causing frustration and unnecessary questions or doubts. God welcomes our fervent prayers, requests, and pleadings for the things that matter to us, but He makes the final call.

We cannot manhandle God, but we can move Him, and the very best way I have found to be in alignment with God's call for my children is to pray His Word. It isn't the only right way to pray, but it is a powerful way to pray. I shared about why I believe so much in praying this way in my book *Praying Mom* . . .

Two truths led me to praying Scripture as my main vehicle of conversation with God.

The first is from Hebrews 4:12, which says the Word of God is "living and effective and sharper than any double-edged sword. . . . It is able to judge the thoughts and intentions of the heart." The second is from Isaiah 55:11: "So my word that comes from my mouth will not return to me empty, but it will accomplish what I please and will prosper in what I send it to do." If those two verses were true, . . . then it seemed to me that there could be no better thing to pray than God's Word itself! . . .

Any time we don't know what to pray, how to pray, or when to pray, we can simply go to God's Word. . . . It isn't like other books out there. . . .

God's Word will teach you everything you need to know about whatever you're praying for.[2]

Praying God's Word keeps our hearts aligned with God's truth, and that will give us great peace. It serves as a source of wisdom and helps us shepherd our boys on the right path, but prayer isn't just something that reminds us of God's truth, who He is, and what He can do. It is those things, but it is so much more. Prayer moves God. And this is a mystery. Just as there are seemingly contradictory Scriptures that cause us to raise an eyebrow and wonder how they could all be true at the same time, God's sovereign control combined with His invitation to His people to pray makes even the best of theologians scratch their heads. Why would we need to pray if God is in control of everything? And yet, there it is, on the pages of our holy Scripture:

"Pray without ceasing . . ." (1 Thessalonians 5:16–18 ESV).

"Seek his face . . ." (1 Chronicles 16:11).

"Pray for one another . . ." (James 5:16).

"When you pray . . ." (Matthew 6:6–9).

". . . in everything by prayer . . ." (Philippians 4:6–7 ESV).

Clearly God's call, God's invitation, God's will is for His people, for parents, to pray.

I believe prayer is proactive. I believe it is action. A verb. It is doing *something*. Maybe the most important *something* we can do. If prayer were not action, it would be nothing. It would accomplish nothing. Do nothing. Mean nothing. And be worth nothing. Prayer is not passive. It is not a last resort. It is not a cop-out, an excuse, or a way to keep our hands from getting dirty. Prayer is the first and best response of the Christian parent to the challenges, depravity, and difficulties her children will face in this world, because she serves the God who can, does, and reigns.

Prayer is battle.

Prayer is war.

Prayer is action.

Prayer is fighting FOR our sons.

How to Use This Book

The next part of this book, part 1, is for you, mom, to prepare your own heart for the battle. I have found over the years that when my heart is leaning toward the Lord, our conversations just flow better. The first chapter contains the prayer I pray most often (like four to five times a day) in my own life. The second chapter is based on an interview with a woman whose wisdom had a profound impact on my own parenting, and I can't wait to share it with you. Both chapters have ten Scripture-inspired prayers to go with them so you can begin praying right away. I know you want to jump right in to praying for your sons, but it's essential to learn to pray for yourself as well. Prayer is, at its core, a relationship with the Lord. Your prayer life will be a rich back-and-forth as you talk to Him about your teen boy. So before you do that, talk to God about your own struggles, needs, and fears.

Start with part 1, return often, and prepare your heart to fight for your teen boy.

The second part of this book includes seven prayer themes to pray for your teen boy. Like the first two chapters, each has ten Scripture-inspired prayers. I've tried to share stories from both my own life and from the Bible to help us all understand why these themes are so important for boys, but I don't want you to only *understand* . . . I want you to *do*. I want you to pray. That's the whole point of this book, so please don't look over those important prayers at the end of each chapter. I've written each chapter in this section with our teen boys in mind, all of them on purpose and with great intention. They don't represent every single thing moms need to pray for their sons. Instead, I hope they'll get you thinking, and that as you pray through them God will show you more areas where your son needs specific prayer.

Pray through one theme each day. Pick a verse or two to dive into deeply. Add an alarm to your phone and pray throughout the day. Pray after you drop your son off at school, over the breakfast table, or as you're going to sleep at night. Ask God to show you what you need to know about those verses in your own life as well as in your son's. I could have picked a lot more than just these seven themes, but I had to stop somewhere. I hope they'll serve as a springboard for God to grow your own prayer life in the future.

You might also ask your teen boy to share an area or two where he thinks he needs prayer right now. Anything to open conversation, right? Ask him to pick and commit to praying in this area for himself every day for ten days, and then ask him for another area. One way to make this easy is to send him the Scriptures and Scripture-inspired prayers at the end of each chapter. You can pray them together, and he doesn't have to think too hard about what to pray. A win for every teenage boy I know.

Before we start praying, I want to quote (with a few changes) what I wrote at the beginning of *Praying for Boys* more than a decade ago. It is just as true for moms of teen boys today . . .

God is FOR you.

This parenting of the male species is hard—whether you have an adventurous boy, a scholarly boy, a rambunctious boy, or a bookworm boy. Whether your boy is married or single, sinner, saved, or sanctified.

START A PRAYING FOR TEEN BOYS PRAYER GROUP

If you have a teenage son, I'm willing to bet you know other moms, grandmothers, or mentors of teen boys. My guess is that they feel very much like you do about parenting those teen boys. In fact, you probably have much more in common with them than you think. Your teen boys might even be what bring you together, and I bet they would love some encouragement and company as they pray for their sons. You could text them, tag them on Facebook, or pull them aside at church or a game and say, "Hey, I'm starting a small group to pray for our teen boys. Want to join?" They will either tell you they don't have time, or they will look relieved and say, "When does it start?" Those are your people. Look for them. The way you run your prayer group is up to you, but I'll suggest a basic plan:

1. Plan to meet at the beginning in person.
2. Send out links to buy the book or buy them for the group yourself.
3. Read one chapter per week for nine weeks.
4. Have a weekly check-in. You can do it in person or on your phone (apps like GroupMe, Marco Polo, WhatsApp, or Voxer are great for this type of communication).
5. Share the names of your teen boys with each other. Pray for one teen boy other than your own each week.
6. Meet at the end of the nine weeks to share what God has done in your lives.
7. Share what you're learning using social media. You can find more encouragement at the @prayingforteenboys Instagram account.
8. Repeat

However you end up using this book, I invite you to commit in your heart right now to continue praying for your son. It's the part of the battle for his heart most overlooked in our culture today, but in truth, there couldn't be anything more important.

It's still hard.

I've watched your words over the years, you boymoms, as you've emailed me, left comments online, or chatted with me over coffee, and I confess: I've been totally overwhelmed for you . . . for me. I've rested my head many nights, speechless that God would allow me to kneel with you and pray for His hand in our boys' lives.

Several times I've asked God, "What are you doing?" And other times I've read about a mom's deep burden for her son and all I could utter was "Oh, God."

He hears our groanings.

The coupled pain and hope that keeps a mama on her knees wears a carpet thin. But He hears you, and He is for you.

You are the apple of His eye. His beloved. His thoughts toward you are many and His plans for you are good. He will never leave you nor forsake you.

When your son takes his first steps into manhood, and you realize that your time is short . . . God is for you.

When you give it your all and he doesn't appreciate it . . . God is for you.

When he walks into the room and you're surprised by the sheer physical presence of him . . . God is for you.

When you realize the home life you desperately wanted to provide for him hasn't happened . . . God is for you.

When you're defeated and ready to quit . . . God is for you.

When you realize that some of the things you don't like about your son are a direct reflection of you . . . God is for you.

When your son gets hurt, doesn't achieve a dream, or is belittled by friends, and you can't protect him . . . God is for you.

When his heart doesn't belong to just you anymore . . . God is for you.

When he makes choices that hurt you . . . God is for you.

When the threads of your carpet are worn bare from the praying, begging, hoping in God to complete the work He started . . . God is for you.

And His heart for you is good.

Promise to remember that? Now, let's start praying.[3]

PART ONE

WHAT TO PRAY FOR
YOURSELF

1

LORD, SHOW ME

His heart was all laid out in the space between us—not much between the front seats of my SUV—and I didn't know what to do about it. We'd spent the last thirty minutes talking about a challenge he was facing at school, and the question at the tail end of the conversation hung in the air like dead weight. *"What should I do?"*

He didn't know that I'd been silently praying for wisdom the entire trip. Just a short "Lord, show me wisdom . . ." "Lord, show me the right words . . . " sent up to heaven while my boy bared his heart. Fifteen, full of life and, unfortunately, life's challenges, he was asking his mama for her insight—something I didn't want to take for granted—and the reality was that I didn't have an answer.

Thankfully, I knew the God who did.

When I started praying God's Word for my two boys, I made long lists of all the things I wanted God to change about them—their struggles, character flaws, sinful attitudes, and if I'm honest, personality traits—and then searched His Word for matching verses or passages I could pray.

I truly believe in the power of God's Word to change the heart (Hebrews 4:12) and that God's Word will do exactly what He purposes for it (Isaiah 55:11). Combined, these two verses tell me that praying God's Word for our children is the very best parenting plan out there. But what I discovered years ago is that the verses and passages I searched for my children slowly began to do what they do best: change me. As we all know, when you change one variable in an equation, the outcome changes as well.

Prayer is a long game. After faithfully praying Scripture over my sons for years—for many things I am only just now beginning to see answers—we still have a long way to go. The more visible response to my prayers is the work of growth and maturity God has done in me. I'm not the same Brooke I was ten years ago, and by God's grace, I won't be the same Brooke ten years into the future. As we mature in our faith and walk with God, it will change how we interact with our children. I'm happy to say that I look more like the mom I wanted to be when they were young.

I like to think I know a little something about boys. God positioned me uniquely with one older brother, a father who was one of three boys, and a husband who was also one of three boys. Then, after I naively prayed for the opportunity to raise boys of my own, God blessed me with two of them, born just twenty-three months apart. They rocked my world. And by that, I mean they kicked my feet out from under me in all the best ways. Of course, it didn't feel good at the time. It felt terrible! But God used my boys, my rambunctious, difficult to manage, 250 percent boys to strip me of my pride and show me how much I needed Him. Not just for salvation, but for every moment of every day.

Because God was teaching me so much, and because I tend to be a teacher myself, I started sharing about what I was learning through parenting boys publicly on a small mom blog. Soon after that, I met the woman who would be my business and ministry partner for over twelve years. Together, we had five boys, and so we combined our efforts and created an online space just for moms of boys called The MOB (Mothers of Boys) Society. Our hearts were to curate information and resources to help moms raise godly men, and prayer was the sturdy foundation upon which we built everything. I began leading other boymoms in how to search the Scriptures for verses and passages to pray for their sons, and it became one of the hallmark offerings of our community.

I believe prayer is one of the most overlooked parts of Christian parenting. Soon after we created The MOB Society, God gave me the privilege of writing about the importance of prayer in my very first book, *Praying for Boys: Asking God for the Things They Need Most*. It helped moms learn to pray God's Word over their sons in areas like obedience, integrity, pride, honor, and overcoming fears, and it was directed more toward moms of younger boys. I loved that book. I still love that book, but as my boys grew into young men, I realized that I had learned so much more about praying for boys that could help moms of teens navigate this new, challenging season with grace.

In 2019, I pivoted and started a new ministry based solely on trying to help moms learn to pray. Million Praying Moms became my passion, at least in part because of the work God did in me as I learned to pray for my own two boys. Our mission is to help moms see prayer not as a last resort, but as the first and best response to the challenges of motherhood, and my desire is to help every mom I encounter understand the gift she's been given in the privilege of partnering with God in prayer for her kids.

That day in the car, as I drove to baseball practice with my then fifteen-year-old son and listened to him spill his heart about the challenges he was facing, I had a revelation. In spite of all my experience with boys, I really didn't know what to do, or how to help him fix the problem he had. But as he talked, and I listened, I prayed a very simple prayer: *Show me. Show me.* And God did. Not right away. I distinctly remember having to tell my son in the car that I needed to think and pray about the situation before giving him an answer. But since that first simple *show me* prayer, I can honestly say there has never been a time when I've asked God for wisdom for my children that He hasn't given it. Liberally.

Sometimes He's given me wisdom right in the moment. More often, I've had to keep praying *show me* as I searched His Word or talked to a friend. But God's wisdom does cry aloud in the street, and if we listen and look, her voice can be heard above all the noise and commotion and emotion of the circumstances we face (Proverbs 1:20). Moreover, God promises to give us wisdom if we'll only ask for it (James 1:5), and I have always found Him to be a Man of His Word.

When you and I ask God to *show me*, we're asking Him to *show me* His wisdom, to *show me* the next right step, *show me* His plan, *show me* what to say, *show me* what He's doing, and *show me* where to go. In short, we're asking Him to help us see the things we can't currently see. And there's a lot we can't see.

Thankfully, our God makes the hidden things known (Daniel 2:22). He will reveal to you the things that are influencing your son's life that, perhaps, he hasn't shared with you. He is the God who makes a way where there seems to be no way (Isaiah 43:19) and will help you and your family put one foot in front of the other. He is the God who loves your child more than you do (John 3:16) and whose plans for him are good (Jeremiah 29:11). He is that God, and all of this is available to you and me as we invite God into the challenges of motherhood through prayer. Yes, the *show me* prayer is my most frequent prayer.

Why? Because frankly, there's just so much I don't know.

The Old Testament story of the parents of Samson highlights the way they found out about their unexpected son. After years of enduring the shame and humiliation of barrenness, Manoah and his wife were visited by an angel who told them their special son would be a Nazarite and gave them instructions for his care. To be a Nazarite meant to be set apart, usually for a specific time, to fulfill a specific plan of the Lord. But in Samson's case, he was to be a Nazarite for his entire life, and not only was *he* to be set apart for the Lord, so was his mom. (Interestingly, when the angel, whom some commentaries say might actually have been Christ Himself, announced the birth of Samson, he spoke first to Manoah's wife and gave her directions for how she would influence her son while he was still in the womb. With that simple act, the angel recognized and validated the importance of a mother's influence on her son. I love that.) The angel told the couple that she had to abstain from alcohol and unclean food and that they could never cut Samson's hair.

Manoah's response? Look at Judges 13:8: "Manoah prayed to the LORD and said, 'Please, Lord, let the man of God you sent come again to us and teach us what we should do for the boy who will be born.'"

Did you catch that? The man who raised Samson—the prophet all children who attend Sunday school learn about as the strongest man who ever lived—begged the Lord to show him how to raise his son! Manoah's heart . . . isn't it just like ours? Don't we have that same question? Don't we wish an angel of the Lord would visit us and show us what to do?

My boys are being raised in a way that is almost totally different from the way I was raised. Not when it comes to morals and values. Not when it comes to teaching them to love the Lord. We are trying hard to raise our children in a Christian home that stands on the solid rock of Jesus Christ, even in this difficult culture. But our children are experiencing their culture in a completely different way than my husband and I did because of developments in technology. Bullies existed when I was in school. But now, those bullies are recording kids making stupid mistakes, or compromised in vulnerable situations, and spreading the video everywhere in a matter of seconds via social media. Just last week, my younger son told me about something crazy a friend of his did at a sleepover that was recorded and shared all over the school.

I used to come home at night or on the weekends and get a safe and loving reprieve from the stressors at school. Even if I chose to do something stupid at a sleepover, there was no documented proof! Now, those stressors (and bullies) follow our children home in their pockets in the form of a smartphone. When I say there's just so much I don't know, I don't mean the heart-level issues. I'm referring to the many ways there are today to express the issues of the heart that didn't even exist when I was a teenager. It can be overwhelming, and I've seen more than one well-meaning parent tap out and give up because it just seems too hard.

But I don't think God is calling us to give up.

I think He's calling us to press in, to ask for help, and pray like Manoah, *show me*. As I have shared previously,

> Maybe you and I weren't visited by an angel of the Lord to announce the births of our sons, but the call of God is no less evident on their lives. Maybe our sons won't have supernatural physical strength designed to defeat entire armies alone, but they *will* be called on to fight the enemy of their souls on a daily basis. And maybe the story of our sons' lives will only be known to a few instead of many, but the impact their lives can have on those around them is no less profound.[1]

Prayer—asking the Lord to show us what we need to know, in addition to praying His Word proactively over their lives—is one of the most important gifts we can give to our sons in the teenage years, because there is so much out there that can lead them astray. There is an enemy whose entire plan for them is to "steal and kill and destroy" (John 10:10), and it's in our best interests as parents to take that seriously.

When our younger son was just ten years old, he was invited to a birthday party where he was, quite literally, the only child there who didn't have a cell phone. When I picked him up and he told me this, I didn't believe him! How many times did I try to use that excuse with my parents when I wanted something I didn't have? Turns out, he really was the only one there who didn't have one yet (and it was a couple more years before he got one), and of course he couldn't understand why. My husband and I explained to him that it wasn't because we didn't trust him (we did . . . as much as you can trust a ten-year-old). We wanted to wait on giving him a cell phone because we didn't trust other people. Unfortunately, when he was just a decade old, I had to explain evil to my son and help him understand that there are people out there who want to hurt him.

The world is after our children. They will face temptations. They will face opportunity after opportunity to choose what is good, right, and true or what is evil. The Bible promises straight paths for those who seek after Him with their whole hearts (Proverbs 3:5–6), but there is no such promise for those who seek something else. When they're ten, we can make those hard decisions for them. When they're seventeen, that becomes much harder.

His entire senior year of high school, I found myself asking the Lord if we had done enough for our older son. Had we taught our son everything he needed to know? Had we given him a firm enough foundation that he'd be able to stand tall in the hard world? Were there lessons we still needed to teach so he would be prepared to make the best decisions possible? Had we stressed that following God's plan was the very best way to live?

Of course, the answer was no, we hadn't done enough. I know this because I had excellent parents, and they didn't give me everything I needed either. They did a great job preparing me for adulthood and continued to stand by me as I left their home (and even to this day), but there's no way one set of parents can give a child everything they need in just eighteen years. There will be lessons my sons, and yours, have to learn the hard way. They may very well make some bad decisions, sinful decisions, and decisions they'll later regret. I did. I bet you did too. In some cases, it will seem like the enemy is winning, and the best we can hope for is that they'll rely on what we've taught them to navigate what he attempts to throw their way. But remember, while there will always be limits to what we can do, there will never be limits to what we can pray.

So we must pray, and we must never stop praying. As E. M. Bounds writes, "I think Christians fail so often to get answers to their prayers because they do not wait long enough on God."[2]

In Ephesians chapter 6, the passage that instructs believers on what to do when they are under major spiritual attack, Paul uses the word *stand* three times:

Put on the full armor of God so that you can stand against the schemes of the devil. (v. 11)

Having prepared everything, . . . take your stand. (v. 13)

Stand, therefore, with truth like a belt around your waist. (v. 14)

So stand. Don't quit. Refuse to give up. Be bold and ask God: *Show me.* "We should give the Lord no rest until we see fruit. Therefore, in persevering yet submissive prayer, we should make our requests known to God."[3] Make your requests known.

Mom, be willing to make yourself a vessel for the Lord to help birth His plan for your son through your prayers. Believe Him. Ask Him. Ask Him again. Make *show me* your constant prayer *for you,* expecting God to give you the wisdom He delights to give at just the right time.

"LORD, SHOW ME" PRAYERS

Daniel 2:22—"He reveals the deep and hidden things; he knows what is in the darkness, and light dwells with him."

> **PRAYER:** Father, show me what I need to see. Reveal the deep and hidden things in _____'s life that may be keeping him from all you have for him. If there is darkness in his heart, move your Holy Spirit to convict. Bring him into your light. In Jesus' name, Amen.

Jeremiah 29:11—"'For I know the plans I have for you'—this is the LORD's declaration—'plans for your well-being, not for disaster, to give you a future and a hope.'"

> **PRAYER:** Lord, I believe you have good plans for _____. Show both of us what those are step-by-step. In Jesus' name, Amen.

Proverbs 3:5–6—"Trust in the LORD with all your heart, and do not rely on your own understanding; in all your ways know him, and he will make your paths straight."

PRAYER: Lord, help me to trust you with the plans you have for
_____ . I'm so tempted to lean on what I can see with
my own eyes, but I know there's much more to your plans than
only that. As we follow you, make his paths straight. In Jesus'
name, Amen.

Deuteronomy 31:8—"The LORD is the one who will go before you. He will be with you; he will not leave you or abandon you. Do not be afraid or discouraged."

PRAYER: Father, go before me, and show me your plans. Be with
me as I lead _____ . Never leave me and help me not to
be afraid or discouraged by what I can see with my own eyes.
In Jesus' name, Amen.

Psalm 32:8—"I will instruct you and show you the way to go;
with my eye on you, I will give counsel."

PRAYER: Lord, see _____ . Keep your eyes on him and
show us the way to go. Instruct us on the right paths. In Jesus'
name, Amen.

John 10:27–28—"My sheep hear my voice, I know them, and
they follow me. I give them eternal life, and they will never
perish. No one will snatch them out of my hand."

PRAYER: Lord, help me to let go of all distractions so that I can
hear your voice. Help me to know your voice better than I know
my own so I can follow you. Keep me and _____ firmly
in your hand. In Jesus' name, Amen.

Romans 8:28—"We know that all things work together for
the good of those who love God, who are called according to
his purpose."

PRAYER: Lord, work all of the things happening in _____'s life right now together for your good. Help me believe you are working ALL things—good and bad—together for your purpose. In Jesus' name, Amen.

Ecclesiastes 3:1—"There is an occasion for everything, and a time for every activity under heaven."

PRAYER: Father, help me to remember that there is more to _____'s life than just now. This is a season, and there will be another. Lead me in leading him well where we are right now. In Jesus' name, Amen.

Proverbs 19:21—"Many plans are in a person's heart, but the LORD's decree will prevail."

PRAYER: Father, move in _____'s heart so that he desires your will above all else, and help me to desire it too, especially when I can't see you at work. In Jesus' name, Amen.

Psalm 27:14—"Wait for the LORD; be strong, and let your heart be courageous. Wait for the LORD."

PRAYER: Father, help me to wait on you. Give me the strength to believe you're in complete control of _____'s life, and the courage to keep coming to you for guidance. In Jesus' name, Amen.

PRAYERS AND NOTES

2

LORD, HELP ME KEEP HIS HEART

When I was in my early twenties, I had the privilege of over-seeing a volunteer-driven parenting program that reached out to local women, helping them learn the basics of motherhood while also providing them with material resources to ease their financial burden. I wasn't a teacher in the program, but when I took the job, I felt it was important to visit every single class personally so that I could vouch for it and make sure we were giving our very best to the women we served. I didn't have children myself in that season, so I approached one particular class in the program with great curiosity. I don't remember its exact name, but it was basically Biblical Parenting 101, and leading the class was a seasoned mother and grandmother named Ruth Anne Roberts.

Ruth Anne had volunteered at the Pregnancy Resource Center where we held the program for many years by the time I got there . . . a household name if you will. She had children of her own, grown and out in the world serving. Her hands were starting to bend with arthritis, but her heart and mind blazed brilliantly as she shared what she believed to be the foundations of biblical parenting.

I wish I had recorded her sessions, because I don't remember much at all about the details she shared. Not because her teaching wasn't good or couldn't capture my attention, but because she shared one thought at the beginning of the class that so grabbed my heart there was no room left for anything else.

"Keep their hearts."

Those three words captivated me. I rolled them around in my mind and heart over and over again as she spoke, and thought, *This. This is what parenting is about. If I can learn to keep the hearts of my children . . . if God can help me do this . . . I can be a good mom.*

Whenever I share Ruth Anne's philosophy with other people (which she says came from a book she read, but that we couldn't find), they want more details. What does it mean to keep the hearts of your children? How does it work? What does it look like? It's been twenty or more years since I first heard Ruth Anne share those words, so I decided to reach out to her and see if there was a way to meet with her and get her perspective on those questions. I wasn't sure about the status of her health. She was in her mid-60s when we first met, which made her eighty-six when I walked into her home to interview her. I was thrilled to see that she is still able to live at home and do everything she wants to do. She still even mows her yard . . . although I told her if we lived closer I would insist on making my boys do that for her. Her beloved husband went to be with the Lord several years ago, and our time together found her still faithfully serving in her local church, teaching a women's Bible study. I adore her, and I'm so glad we got to spend this time together. What follows is a mixture of her wisdom and mine on learning to keep our children's hearts.

There Is No Formula

I have found that Christian parents deeply desire a formula for raising godly kids, and as a Christian parent myself, I completely understand why. I've often said to the Lord, "Just show me what to do and I'll do it!" We want to be obedient and please the Lord in our parenting, but there's no manual I've been able to find that explains Christian child-rearing step-by-step that produces a good, solid, devoted Christian every single time. I've known too many children of mature Christian parents who don't walk with the Lord, and too many children of non-Christians who do, to believe such a manual exists. If it did, we'd all be following it, and there would be considerably fewer children leaving the church when they turn eighteen.

So when I endeavor to explain this idea that provided a foundation for my own parenting, and that I've prayed for my own children since they were very young, I like to start here: It isn't a formula; it's a perspective based on biblical truth. The formula that does hold true is that parenting is really the sum total of all our brokenness, plus our sinful humanity, plus what we know about God, plus what we know about the world, plus what we know about our child *in that moment*. All a mother can ever do is the very best she knows *in the moment* to honor the Lord with her children. I'm not promising that praying for God to help you keep the hearts of your children will produce kids who love the Lord. What I am saying is that it can help, and that even if they choose a different path for a while, building a solid relationship with them will carry you through.

Love Them Harder than They Fight You

God did not give me compliant boys. As I stated in the introduction, when they were young they were quite the handful. They fought me a lot, and I quickly found that normal corrections didn't work with them. There was no "time out mat" that would hold them. They wouldn't stay in their rooms, and physical punishment didn't even seem to create a bump in the road. All it did was separate me from them emotionally, so I gave it up for other forms of correction that were more effective at reaching their hearts.

They weren't bad boys. Actually, they were incredibly loving and affectionate while also being noncompliant . . . if that can be a thing. It probably helped balance things in our home and kept me deeply connected to them even when they brought me to my knees, so I'm grateful, but the early years with them were fraught with tears and chaos, and I was constantly overwhelmed. I had no idea how to make them behave and routinely felt like a failure. I was convinced they would turn out to be complete heathens if we couldn't get a handle on their aggressive, impulsive, energetic personalities. I routinely got calls from Sunday school teachers asking what to do with their incredibly high energy levels, and my reply was always the same: "When you figure it out, let me know."

As I've cried out to the Lord in desperation, God has given me several revelations, or goals, in handling my hard-to-handle boys to help build relationships with them instead of tear them down (check out my Fight Like a Boymom course for a deeper dive into this). One of the goals that has meant the most to me is that I endeavor to love my boys harder than they fight me. This, I believe, is the heartbeat of keeping the hearts of our children. If, at the end of the day, our children can go to sleep safe and secure in the love of their parents, it's a win because it keeps and restores the relationship.

This goal of mine applied when they were little and physically fought me, and it applies now, when they're teenagers trying to find their own way. Just the other day one of my children got in trouble in school. I got the dreaded call from the principal's office telling me he had done something against the rules and would be punished for it. I listened intently, with total respect for the authority God has placed over my children in their schools, trying my best to reserve judgment until I could hear my son's side of the story. And when he got in the car that afternoon, body slumped over in defeat and frustration, expecting the worst, I looked at him and said, "There's nothing you could ever do to make me not love you. I may not like you right now, but I love you . . . so let's start there. Nothing will ever take away my love."

Our children need to know that even when they mess up, they're safe in the love of their parents. Even when we have to correct or punish them, it should come from a place of love. I can't tell you how many times I've said those same words to our sons over the years: "There's nothing you could ever do to make me not love you." I say it over and over again because I want them to KNOW it deep down in their knower. There's nothing. NOTHING. Nothing. I will love them harder than they fight me, harder than they fight their father, and harder than they might choose to fight God. Harder.

And isn't that how God loves us?

It's God's kindness that leads us to repentance (Romans 2:4), not His wrath. His love—His desire for relationship with His creation—is what woos us to Him and births in us the desire to please Him. When I heard Ruth Anne share those words all those years ago, this truth informed my understanding. Woo your children. Be kind to your children. Make every effort to keep their hearts turned toward you, and love them harder than they fight you. Make it your goal to love them in a way that sustains relationship and makes it so they want to please you rather than go their own way.

My home is not perfect. There have been times when we've missed the mark, chosen the wrong path, and acted in ways that weren't very loving toward each other. There have been times when we've chosen to go our own ways instead of toward each other. My boys have drastically different personalities and life experiences, even though they've been raised in the same home. But they've both been loved hard, and that hard love usually brings their hearts home to us, even if it takes some time.

Let Them Get to Know the Jesus in You

There's a sign in my kitchen that says "Please excuse the chaos. I suck as a housewife." It's more accurate than I'd like it to be. I tend to react more quickly than I'd like, and I always regret it when I do. When I'm stressed, my habit is to retreat into a book or binge *Gilmore Girls* reruns instead of giving my people the attention they deserve. And I can be sarcastic. On the "speak the truth in love" scale (Ephesians 4:15), I fall squarely on truth and have to work to balance it with love. I'm far from perfect, as my husband or either son will happily tell you, but I do think I've gotten a few things right over the years. Prayer is one of them. Loving hard is another. I'm also halfway decent at turning life experiences into life lessons, connecting the dots from the struggles and joys my children experience to some truth about God's character or how He acts and moves in the world. Actually, I'm probably annoying about it, but I believe that it not only helps my children learn to apply God's truths to their lives themselves (a skill all Christians should aspire to have) but also gets them to know *me* as a woman of God, and that's important.

Growing up, I only saw my mom as "my mom." I undervalued her as a woman and as a woman of God. I was selfish in my demands of her and thought she existed only to serve me. I know better now, and my hope is that by approaching all of life as an opportunity to talk about the God I know, love, and serve, I'll allow my boys to know me outside of just being their mom, and at some point they'll respect me for being a child of God. I hope knowing what's going on in my head will help them consider what they believe about God and never have to wonder what I think about God. I want them to see God in me, something Ruth Anne also suggested.

By inviting our sons into our personal relationship with Christ, we can give them insight into ourselves and invite them to ponder their own relationship with God. After all, they are our brothers in Christ, not just our sons, and as they get older and our relationship changes and matures, this part of our relationship will become more and more valuable.

For it to work, though, we have to be willing to share our doubts and fears along with our confidence and trust. Teenagers can smell a fake a mile away, and there's no relationship that's more potentially fragrant than a parent trying to cover what they don't know or understand. We must be honest. If we don't get it, we should tell them we don't get it. If we don't know the answer, we need to tell them we don't know and that we'll try to find it for them. Sometimes we will be able to, and sometimes we'll have to admit that there's no answer to be found this side of heaven. But our relationship will grow as we work these things out together, and our boys will respect us more when we're honest. Living this way helps us give each other grace, and that's a key component in maintaining relationship, or keeping their hearts.

Give and Receive Grace Freely

The reality is that we will get things wrong as parents, and grace is for us as much as it is for our children. I joke about the kind of housewife I am, but the wisdom that has served me well here is to ask for grace from my children (and husband) when I need it and extend it in turn to them as much as I can. I have asked my children for forgiveness many, MANY times since I became a mom, and I'm sure I will countless times more before they're grown.

Parenting is probably the biggest work of patience there is, both as we wait for God to do a work in our kids, and as we wait for Him to continue to do the work He started in us. Meshing all of that human imperfection together with immaturity and sin requires nothing short of amazing amounts of grace, and aren't we happy that God gave it to us first? If you struggle to give grace, remember how much you need it, not just for your salvation, but for every moment of every day.

Be With Them

This one can be tough, especially in today's culture, when it's so easy for kids (and their parents, ahem) to walk around with their noses stuck in a device of some kind. I have seen people run into walls and tables, as well as trip over otherwise easy-to-see obstacles because they were walking around looking at a screen. In Ruth Anne's parenting days, you were more likely to see a child walking around with their nose in a book, but one of the things she stressed to me that seemed to be vital to the success of the relationship she had with her children was a concerted effort to be with them.

She said, "We tried to be interested in what they were interested in, and we gave them opportunity as we could to be involved in our lives too." She had a specific memory of her husband, Jim, playing on the floor with their girls and their dollhouse. I played with a lot of monster trucks when my boys were young, building dirt ramps on baseball fields while my husband played on the church softball team. He often took the boys to a large field near our first home where they could run and chase each other, ride bikes around the track, or hit a baseball off the tee. We watched *The Sandlot* over and over and over again because it was *their* favorite movie (and now we can all quote entire scenes by heart).

Now that they're teenagers, this translates into trying to love what they love, even if we don't initially get it. A couple of years ago, my baseball-loving son decided to love basketball. I have never loved basketball, and I was a little bit disappointed in his decision at first . . . until I saw him start to excel and realized how much he truly loves it. I began to try to figure it out beyond the basics, bought basketball T-shirts to take the place of my baseball tees, and planted my rear in the gym for every game. We even bought him a really nice basketball hoop for his sixteenth birthday so he could "hoop" in our driveway. We invested our time, energy, and money in what was important to him. If we'd insisted on trying to get him to stick with what we loved, we would've missed an opportunity to bond with him and show him he's important to our family. That's the kind of message we don't want to send if we hope to have a relationship with our sons built on trust and respect.

My ultimate prayer is that our efforts to keep our children's hearts extend into the relationships they have with their heavenly Father. It's so much easier to relate to God as a loving father when we have that love modeled to us by our parents. It isn't impossible for God to teach our kids to know and love Him in the absence of a strong parental relationship, but why not give our kids the foundation they need to make the leap from loving us to loving God? Ultimately, it's His job to keep them, and that's what we'll talk about next.

"LORD, HELP ME KEEP HIS HEART" PRAYERS

Numbers 6:24–26 (ESV)—"The LORD bless you and keep you; the LORD make his face to shine upon you and be gracious to you; the LORD lift up his countenance upon you and give you peace."

> **PRAYER:** Lord, bless _____ and keep him. Make your face to shine upon him and be gracious to him. Give him the light of your favor and bless him with your peace. In Jesus' name, Amen.

Ephesians 6:2–3—"Honor your father and mother, which is the first commandment with a promise, so that it may go well with you and that you may have a long life in the land."

> **PRAYER:** Father, help _____ choose to honor the authority you've placed in his life. As he does, grant him wellness and a long life. In Jesus' name, Amen.

First Peter 4:8—"Above all, maintain constant love for one another, since love covers a multitude of sins."

> **PRAYER:** Father, help me to love _____ harder than he fights me, allowing the love you've given me for him to cover a multitude of sins. In Jesus' name, Amen.

First Thessalonians 5:11—"Therefore encourage one another and build each other up as you are already doing."

> **PRAYER:** Lord, give me the ability to encourage and build up _____. Help me have the right words to reach his heart. In Jesus' name, Amen.

Ephesians 4:29—"No foul language should come from your mouth, but only what is good for building up someone in need, so that it gives grace to those who hear."

> **PRAYER:** Father, help me to recognize when _____ is in need, and give me the right words to extend your grace to him to build him up. In Jesus' name, Amen.

Proverbs 13:20—"The one who walks with the wise will become wise, but a companion of fools will suffer harm."

> **PRAYER:** Lord, bring _____ wise friends. May he be drawn to wisdom and repelled by foolishness. In Jesus' name, Amen.

James 1:19–20—"My dear brothers and sisters, understand this: Everyone should be quick to listen, slow to speak, and slow to anger, for human anger does not accomplish God's righteousness."

> **PRAYER:** Lord, give _____ and me the ability to approach each other with understanding. Make us quick to listen, slow to speak, and slow to anger. In Jesus' name, Amen.

Colossians 3:23—"Whatever you do, do it from the heart, as something done for the LORD and not for people."

> **PRAYER:** Father, teach _____ to do everything as if he's doing it for you, and give each task the honor it deserves. In Jesus' name, Amen.

Hebrews 10:24—"And let us consider one another in order to provoke love and good works."

PRAYER: Lord, help our family to be considerate of one another, looking for ways to provoke each other to love and good works. In Jesus' name, Amen.

First Peter 5:6–7—"Humble yourselves, therefore, under the mighty hand of God, so that he may exalt you at the proper time, casting all your cares on him, because he cares about you."

PRAYER: Father, help us to humbly cast all of our cares on you, because you care for us. In Jesus' name, Amen.

PRAYERS AND NOTES

PART TWO

WHAT TO PRAY FOR YOUR TEEN BOY

3

LORD, KEEP HIS HEART

I heard the alarm go off from the kitchen as I prepared breakfast before the boys left for school, but there was no movement from the occupant of the second door on the left down the hall. I hadn't expected there to be. A heavy sleeper, he routinely slept through his alarm and needed someone to wake him up so he wouldn't be late for school. It often took a few attempts before he finally moved. I knew the time was coming when he would need to learn to wake up on his own but had decided that today wasn't the day. My desire to be the first person to see him in the morning, brush the hair away from his forehead, and talk to God about him before his feet hit the floor was too strong to be ignored. It was a habit I treasured enough that I was willing to baby him in this area through his senior year in high school (and I promise, he does a fine job of waking himself up in college). So I set my cup of steaming coffee on the counter, walked down the hall, opened his door, sat beside him on his warm bed, placed my hand on his head, and began to pray . . . silently . . .

Lord, keep him. Remember him today. When the world throws more at him than is fair, help him think of you and ask for help. When the enemy tries to tempt him, help him to stand strong. Bring his mind intentionally to settle on the truths we've tried to hide in his heart over the years. May they come to him at just the right times today. Hang on tightly and don't let go. In Jesus' name, Amen.

In the last chapter, we talked about the foundational goal of keeping a strong relationship between parent and child. Now I want to spend some time talking about the more important relationship of our son's life—the one between him and his God.

It might catch some parents off guard to say that there's any relationship more important than the one between parent and child. Certainly it is an extremely important one, setting the tone in undeniable ways for the duration of our children's lives. But I hope to help us look beyond that and see how the relationship we have with our children is only a springboard for something greater. In fact, all of the work we do to keep the hearts of our children points to a much, much bigger spiritual truth: If we can manage to keep the hearts of our children, it will be much easier for them to offer their hearts to God in the same way.

Proverbs 4:23 says, "Guard your heart above all else, for it is the source of life." According to this verse, the heart is the source of life, like a well that provides life-giving water . . . the "center of one's inner life and orientation to God, from which a person does all thinking, feeling, and choosing,"[1] and if the well water gets dirty, it isn't long before people start getting sick.

Matthew Henry says, "There are many ways of keeping things—by care, by strength, by calling in help, and we must use them all in keeping our hearts. . . . We must keep our hearts with more care and diligence than we keep any thing else."[2]

The teen years can feel like one fiery trial after another, with attacks from the enemy around every corner. Sometimes our boys will suffer because of it. Sometimes they'll suffer for living godly lives, and other times for their own sinful choices. As they walk through those fiery trials, God "will allow you to be put you into a situation that only He can get you out of."[3] It's in these times that they can see clearly that He is God, and they will need to be kept through it all.

It's what Jesus modeled in His relationship with the disciples while He walked on earth. Consider John 17:12:

> While I was with them, I kept them in your name, which you have given to me. I have guarded them, and not one of them has been lost (ESV).

Over the course of three years, Jesus walked with His chosen disciples, teaching and leading them to a deeper understanding of God's plan. And while they didn't always understand Him, and quite often made fools of themselves, all but one stayed the course, and that one (Judas) strayed with a heavenly purpose designed to fulfill Scripture. In John 17, we find Jesus praying. In fact, this prayer is referred to as "The High Priestly Prayer" in my Bible and others like it. Jesus was called our "high priest" in Hebrews 5. He was appointed by God to act on our behalf, offering not an animal without blemish, but Himself as our perfect and spotless gift and sacrifice for sin (Hebrews 5:1). It's in this role as our high priest that we find Jesus first praying for His disciples, then praying for those who would become disciples (that's us), and finally, for the strength to continue making His name known, no matter the personal cost. And in the midst of that glorious, rich prayer in John 17, Jesus tells His Father that He "kept" those who had been given to Him, the disciples.

In the *Christian Standard Bible* (CSB), this verse reads, "While I was with them, I was protecting them by your name that you have given me. I guarded them and not one of them is lost." I think this gives us the right perspective for understanding what it means to ask God to keep our children's hearts. When we pray "Lord, keep him," what we're really asking God to do is to protect our sons by the power of His own name. We're asking Him to guard them and not let them get lost.

Again, there's no formula here. What I'm sharing with you doesn't have guaranteed results, but it does pave the way for God's Spirit to be at work in our kids. It's God who changes hearts of stone to hearts of flesh (Ezekiel 36:26), but we can pray for the keeping of their hearts. Let's dive in and figure out what it means to pray for God to keep our children's hearts in three main areas:

- Keep his heart pure
- Keep his heart soft
- Keep his heart clean

Keep His Heart Pure

Both of my children react harshly to poison ivy, and it's weird, because my husband and I do not. We both practically grew up in the woods, rolling and jumping and even sitting in what was presumably at least partially poison ivy. Neither of us have ever had a reaction to it, but our children struggle with it every summer. My nephew was baptized in the New River at a campground in our town. After the baptism the church held a massive picnic celebration, and because they had rented the space for the day, there were kids running around everywhere, including mine. My older son, in particular, was never able to resist climbing a good tree and did so with abandon that afternoon. A few hours into the picnic, one of the dear women of the church who had poured the gospel into me growing up came to me and said, "Brooke, is Max allergic to poison ivy?" Quickly, I said yes and began looking around for him. "You might want to get him down out of that tree," she said, pointing to where he was, in fact, in the process of shimmying all the way up. "It's got the stuff wrapped all the way around it. I bet it's even going to be on his face."

Sure enough, it was all over him. He was completely covered in the stuff. He's reacted to poison ivy so many times in his life that I'd learned how to take care of it at home most of the time without needing to go to the doctor, but not that day. His whole face was beet red, and it had spread from his hands to his legs to his stomach before I even knew what had happened. It's a wonder it didn't get in his eyes. The only remedy was prescription-strength steroid cream and several days of misery in which he learned a valuable lesson . . . poison ivy has three shiny leaves. Three shiny leaves—bad.

One minute, my son was having the time of his life. The next, he was in agony. Poison ivy is deceptive. It can even look pretty, especially in the fall in our part of the world. It turns red and looks almost attractive, but if you're allergic, it's best to stay away.

So it is with sin. My son was young when this happened, and we were able to deal with it easily, but as they get older, the things that can attack our children and hurt them get more costly, are harder to deal with, and have more lasting consequences.

To be pure means to not be mixed or adulterated with any other substance or material, to be free of contamination, to be morally clean, or to be without sin. In the Old Testament, it meant being emptied out or being physically clean, such as the time after a woman's cycle in which she had to purify herself before coming back into the community, or the time after someone touched a dead body, came into contact with a skin disease, or had a baby. These things were understood to make a person "unclean," and the Jewish people had rituals that purified them so they could live normal lives again. All it takes is a brief reading of the book of Leviticus to understand just how important purity was for God's people, and it continues to be so today. In the 1990s, many Christians opted in to what was called "purity culture," intending to empower their children to keep themselves "pure" for marriage, but that's only a small piece of what we're talking about here. Purity goes well beyond whether or not someone is a virgin when they get married. Purity is a state of the heart toward God, a desire not to defile ourselves by sinning against Him.

"How can a young man keep his way pure?" Psalm 119:9 asks. "By keeping your word" is the answer. The only way our sons can keep their hearts pure is by choosing not to sin. And the only way they can have the strength to choose not to sin is by loving God more than they love their sin. I shared it this way in *Everyday Prayers for Peace*: "When I was in my twenties, I was trying to overcome a particular sin and failing over and over. I remember thinking and praying a lot about this process, until finally, I had to admit that I *wanted* to sin. That was the real problem. I kept putting myself in a situation where I had to face this sin because I *wanted* to. More than that, I *loved* my sin. I was running toward it" instead of toward God.[4] Preston Perry said we have to "do the necessary things . . . to not put ourselves in positions where we will have to choose sin over righteousness,"[5] and he's right. I was doing the exact opposite, and it revealed the true state of my heart. My loves were out of order, and God was kind enough to show it to me. May He also do that for our sons.

Keep His Heart Soft

My first Scripture-inspired prayer was based on Ezekiel 36:26. I'd been studying it for some reason that I can't recall now and was struck with a specific truth it revealed that applied to my life as a mom. I've said it before in my other books, and I said it earlier in this chapter, but it is worth repeating here: God is the one who changes hearts of stone to hearts of flesh. As parents, our job is to make it as easy as possible for our sons to know that there is a God who loves them, that He sent His Son to die for their sins, and that they need this kind of salvation not just one time. The power of that salvation must be at work in their hearts, growing the fruit of the Spirit in them and keeping their hearts soft and teachable for the entirety of their lives.

I'm not a proponent of raising weak men, but I do love a good, soft man. *Meek* was the word used to describe the countenance of Jesus Himself, and that simply means not being self-willed or continually concerned with his own way. In a word, *humble*. Philippians 2:3–4 says, "Do nothing out of selfish ambition or conceit, but in humility consider others as more important than yourselves. Everyone should look not to his own interests, but rather to the interests of others." That makes you think of a "soft" man in a little different light, doesn't it? Do we want our boys to become men of understanding, men who care deeply about others, men who have servants' hearts, and men who desire the best for those around them as much as they want it for themselves? Those things don't come naturally. They have to be taught, modeled, and prayed for.

A Christian ministry once asked to interview both me and my husband about our marriage. My husband really doesn't participate in my ministry except to support me in it. He's a strong believer, but he isn't a writer or speaker. He can barely work a computer, so most of what I do, beyond putting words on a page, is a mystery to him. In spite of the fact that he has no public presence in what I do, we agreed to the interview. When they called, the representative from the ministry asked me to share about the way my husband leads me. I told them he leads me by serving our family well. He sacrifices over and over for our well-being, giving of himself much better than I do in return. He sees things that need to be done and does them just to make life easier for me. When the kids were little, he took them so I could get peace and quiet to write and think. He is the behind-the-scenes guy whose job goes mostly unnoticed, but without whom I wouldn't be able to function. Our marriage is an example of Christ and the church because of how sacrificially he serves me.

Unfortunately, the Christian ministry didn't like that answer, and I'm not sure why, because what I shared IS a beautiful picture of the kind of men we hope and pray our boys will become.

Keep His Heart Clean

Despite our best efforts, our boys will mess up. They'll say and do the wrong thing, make us look like bad moms, and hurt our feelings. At times, they'll make us wonder if we did anything right at all, and in those times, the enemy who is just as real for us as he is for our sons will try to beat us down. It might sound something like this:

You're a failure. Everything you've worked so hard for, tried so hard to do well, has failed. You've dedicated your entire life to this boy believing God would show up, and now look. It wasn't enough. It's over. Everything was a lie and there is no hope.

I know that might sound harsh, but I write those words authentically because it's what the voice of the enemy sounds like in my own ears. In fact, the enemy of my soul takes it even a step further and often berates me with these words:

You've staked your entire motherhood on praying to a God who doesn't listen . . . doesn't see you . . . doesn't care. How could you ever have believed that prayer would work? You should have done more. You put your trust in something that accomplishes nothing, and you led thousands of moms astray who trusted what you said.

That one really sucks the life out of me. The visual that forms in my mind when he begins assailing me with words like these is a frazzled mom who has tried so hard cowering in the corner as fiery darts hit her sensitive, raw skin.

But we must stand up, friends. When the enemy assails, we must remember that the prayer of a righteous mom avails. James 5:16 says, "The effectual fervent prayer of a righteous man availeth much" (KJV). Somehow our prayers help usher in the plans of God for our sons, both now and for the future. Maybe it's the mystery to this, so many things about prayer we don't understand, that makes it easy for the enemy to weasel his way in and cause us to doubt, but the only way I've found to fight off the fiery darts is with the truth. As moms, we need to not only pray the truth over ourselves, but also over our sons, and when they mess up, it's more important than ever.

Psalm 51 was written by King David, who had royally messed up (pun intended). He participated in murder, adultery, and deceit; tried to cover it all up; and was confronted by the prophet Nathan with his sin. David, whom we'll explore in more depth in another chapter, repented of his sin and prayed a prayer that helped define what needing a clean heart looks like:

Create in me a clean heart, O God, and renew a right spirit within me. Cast me not away from your presence, and take not your Holy Spirit from me. Restore to me the joy of your salvation, and uphold me with a willing spirit.

vv. 10–12 ESV

David didn't pray for a restored reputation. He prayed for a restored relationship. He saw the reality of his corruption and the depth of his sin and begged God for forgiveness. Sin makes us dirty and separates us from God. David needed to be cleaned up and renewed. As moms, it's easy to worry about how our son's choices make us look to our communities. I have felt that onslaught of pressure and emotion many times (because, as I said, ALL boys will mess up . . . mine have many times), but I want us to choose to fight it. It isn't the most important thing to have a spotless reputation. In fact, I suspect that if we worry more about our reputation than our son's heart, we'll lose our son's heart.

The final piece I love about David's response in this passage is that he knew—and freely admitted—he needed God's help to restore and clean up his heart. As we pray for God to keep our son's hearts clean, we aren't praying for a cleanup on the outside. We aren't trying to raise Pharisees who look like Christ-followers to their friends and family but are far from Him on the inside. Our dream, our prayer, is that our children would follow Christ with their whole hearts, with all the glory and mess that will bring, and that God would use the times they mess up to reveal more of Himself to them, growing them into the men He wants them to be.

Lord, Remember Our Sons

When we pray for God to keep the hearts of our sons—keep them pure, keep them soft, keep them clean—we're asking Him to remember them . . . to take action on their behalf. This is the way Samson prayed in Judges 16:28 when "he called out to the Lord, 'Lord God, please remember me. Strengthen me, God, just once more.'" And the way David prayed in Psalm 106:4: "Remember me, Lord, when you show favor to your people.

Come to me with your salvation." This is the way God remembered Noah in Genesis 8:1, by making the waters flooding the earth recede. The way God remembered Rachel's prayer, granting her the gift of a child (Genesis 30:22). And the way God remembered His people Israel over and over again. The New Testament Greek word for *remember* carries with it implied action. We aren't just asking God to think about our sons, but to move on their behalf. Let's pray that for them right now.

Father, inspire our sons to run after you. Give them hearts that long to know you more and follow you closely. Make them sensitive to the conviction and leading of your Holy Spirit, so that when they sin, their heart's desire is to be back in right relationship with you. Remember them, O Lord, and move on their behalf. In Jesus' name.

"LORD, KEEP HIS HEART" PRAYERS

Proverbs 4:23—"Guard your heart above all else, for it is the source of life."

PRAYER: Father, teach _____ to guard his heart against things that could send him on the wrong path. In Jesus' name, Amen.

Matthew 5:8—"Blessed are the pure in heart, for they will see God."

PRAYER: Lord, keep _____'s heart pure, so that he can see and follow God. In Jesus' name, Amen.

Philippians 4:8—"Finally brothers and sisters, whatever is true, whatever is honorable, whatever is just, whatever is pure, whatever is lovely, whatever is commendable—if there is any moral excellence and if there is anything praiseworthy—dwell on these things."

PRAYER: Father, teach my son to dwell on things that are true, honorable, just, pure, lovely, commendable, morally excellent, and praiseworthy. In Jesus' name, Amen.

Ezekiel 36:26—"I will give you a new heart and put a new spirit within you; I will remove your heart of stone and give you a heart of flesh."

PRAYER: Lord, give _____ a new heart and put a new spirit within him. Remove his heart of stone and give him a heart of flesh. In Jesus' name, Amen.

Proverbs 17:10—"A rebuke cuts into a perceptive person more than a hundred lashes into a fool."

PRAYER: Lord, help _____ to be able to handle and embrace loving rebuke. In Jesus' name, Amen.

Colossians 3:12—"Therefore, as God's chosen ones, holy and dearly loved, put on compassion, kindness, humility, gentleness, and patience."

PRAYER: Lord, let _____ know that he is dearly loved by me and by you, and because of that secure love, may he choose to put on compassion, kindness, humility, gentleness, and patience. In Jesus' name, Amen.

James 4:6—"But he gives greater grace. Therefore he says: God resists the proud but gives grace to the humble."

PRAYER: Father, help _____ understand the magnitude of the grace you give, and may that understanding cause him to be humble and not proud. In Jesus' name, Amen.

Proverbs 3:5–6—"Trust in the LORD with all your heart, and do not rely on your own understanding; in all your ways know him, and he will make your paths straight."

PRAYER: May _____ trust in the Lord with all his heart and not rely on his own understanding. In all his ways cause him to know you, and make his paths straight. In Jesus' name, Amen.

Psalm 51:10–12—"God, create a clean heart for me and renew a steadfast spirit within me. Do not banish me from your presence or take your Holy Spirit from me. Restore the joy of your salvation to me, and sustain me by giving me a willing spirit."

PRAYER: Lord, give _____ a clean heart and renew his spirit. Keep him close to you, and make your Holy Spirit active in him. Help him keep the joy of his salvation always before him. In Jesus' name, Amen.

Psalm 24:3–4—"Who may ascend the mountain of the LORD? Who may stand in his holy place? The one who has clean hands and a pure heart, who has not appealed to what is false, and who has not sworn deceitfully."

PRAYER: Lord, give _____ clean hands and a pure heart. Keep him from following what is false, and compel him not to swear deceitfully. In Jesus' name, Amen.

PRAYERS AND NOTES

4

LORD, LET HIM HEAR WISDOM

Of all the areas we'll cover in this book, wisdom is at the top of my list.

When I was a young mom struggling to find the time and mental space to read and enjoy God's Word for myself, a pastor's wife and mom to three girls told me that she survived her children's early years on the Proverbs. She would read one chapter every day, following along with the day of the month, and that was it. I decided that if it was good enough for a pastor's wife, it was good enough for me, so I adopted the habit to get me through that season.

Recently, in an interview, I was asked to share the Bible reading habit that I tend to come back to again and again. Without hesitation, I said, "When I can't figure out what I want to study, or I'm feeling distant from God, or I just don't want to read my Bible in that season, I always go to Psalms or Proverbs." My reasoning is simple: At the end of my life, if all I ever do is read a psalm or a proverb each day, I think I might just turn out to be a wise woman.

The older they get, the more our boys need wisdom too. And not just any wisdom . . . God's wisdom. After salvation, it's the number one thing that will equip them for a life well-lived. It's THE thing for them to get because wisdom will carry them far in this life when talent, expertise, knowledge, and even faith might fail.

Proverbs tells us that wisdom is loud (Proverbs 1:20–23), and that it cries out to the simple, almost begging them to come and learn. For someone like me, who can be emotional, scattered, stubborn, and sometimes blind to what's right in front of her, this is good news. If that description of me also sounded a lot like the teenage boy in your home (stubborn, scattered, blind), let it stand as proof that he needs God's road map for wisdom too.

If you're worried that you might come up a bit short on the right wisdom at the right time for your boy, lay that worry aside. God says in James 1:5, "Now if any of you lacks wisdom, he should ask God—who gives to all generously and ungrudgingly—and it will be given to him." I don't know about you, but the words *generously* and *ungrudgingly* sound hopeful to me. In fact, I can say with complete confidence that there has never been a time when I've needed wisdom from God, and asked Him for it, that He hasn't given it . . . generously.

Step one in praying for wisdom for our sons is to know where to go to get it for ourselves and to be willing to ask for it when we don't have it. Step two is to have a basic understanding of what wisdom is and is not.

The Bible describes two basic types of men—the foolish and the wise. Even just a cursory reading of Psalms and Proverbs shows the contrast between the two quite clearly. "The fool says in his heart, 'There is no God'" (Psalm 53:1) and does as he pleases all his days. The wise man fears the Lord and follows Him (Proverbs 1:7). Now that they're older and making many decisions for themselves, let's encourage our sons to consider what kind of man they want to be—wise or foolish. It's a question that applies to almost every decision or situation they'll face, so it's a good idea to get them in the habit of asking it.

The Psalms and Proverbs serve as the perfect guide, helping us teach them how to make decisions, which paths to take, and how to understand the life God has called us to as believers. (For a free prayer calendar to help you pray through the entire book of Proverbs for your teenager, visit MillionPrayingMoms.com /PrayingForTeens.) I recommend reading through both books often as a family. When my sons were little, I even played the Proverbs set to music in their rooms at night.

The idea is to do our best to root the truths we find in these two wisdom-packed books deeply in the hearts of our sons any way we can. These truths can be applied in real life to help our sons make choices, providing insight and understanding for almost any scenario they'll face. Marriage, parenting, finances, study and work habits, friendships, authority, and the power of the tongue—wisdom for all these things and more can be found in Proverbs, including a baseline definition for what God's wisdom really is.

What Is God's Wisdom?

Proverbs 1:7 says, "The fear of the LORD is the beginning of knowledge; fools despise wisdom and discipline." The beginning seems as good a place to start as any.

In the book of Ecclesiastes, we find the son of David, King Solomon, musing about the meaning of life. Solomon, who wrote many of the chapters in Proverbs, was called the wisest, and richest, man who ever lived (1 Kings 10:23). He had the means to explore and experience life to its fullest extent, and an extra special helping of God's wisdom (1 Kings 3:1–15), so we can trust that he knows what he's talking about. He denied himself nothing—no pleasure, no gift, no desire—and yet still found it all to be "futile and a pursuit of the wind" (Ecclesiastes 2:10–11). And after all of that self-indulgence, the conclusion of his desire to understand life was this: "Fear God and keep his commands" (Ecclesiastes 12:13).

Over the past few years, I've had the privilege of studying the fruit of the Spirit found in Galatians chapter 5 in depth. In my exploration of love, joy, peace, patience, kindness, goodness, faithfulness, gentleness, and self-control, by far the most important thing I've discovered is that the way the world understands these things is very different from their true biblical meaning.

For example, 1 John 4:8 tells us that "God is love." This not only means that God is loving, though He certainly is, it also means that God and love are the same thing. This tells us that without God there can be no real love. He is the Creator of love and therefore has the distinct privilege of defining what it is and how it should look. *His* definition of love is therefore very different from that of the world, and it's our job to make the way we love look like His definition, not to redefine love altogether and say that because God is love anything goes.

So it is with wisdom. God created it. He defines it. And we can't possibly have it if we don't first fear Him. It's just the way it is. It is the fear of the Lord, the deep love for and awe of Him, that will cause us to want to live with wisdom. If we don't have that deep love and awe, we—and our sons—probably won't see His definition of wisdom as important, or even worth knowing.

Tony Evans says, "To live well in a world gone bad, you have to fear the Lord. That is, you have to take God seriously and embrace his kingdom agenda for your life—even when you don't know where it will lead."[1] The harsh reality is that unless our sons know God, it will be hard for them to know wisdom. So we begin at the beginning, asking God to help our sons fear Him, and then we begin unpacking what true biblical wisdom looks like for them in their daily lives, holding it out as the standard of excellence they can grow into.

Wisdom in Practice

My older son graduated from high school and left four days later to play in a collegiate summer baseball program . . . in a different state. We only saw him a few times over the summer before he left again for college, but he did get to come home for the Fourth of July. We do it up big for the Fourth. Our small town has an amazing all-day festival, and there isn't a better place in the world to see fireworks than our backyard. We have the perfect angle to see the ones the town lets off, and the closer it gets to showtime, the more vehicles fill up our yard to see them. We make a day of it, really, inviting friends and family to join us for a potluck cookout and games of whiffle ball and cornhole in the backyard. We even invite the musicians from a local old-time music group to play all day long so our guests can catch up, play, and eat with the rich cultural history of our region playing in the background.

It's fun.

But this particular Fourth of July was also a bit stressful. Our son had called a few days earlier with the news that his college baseball plans were changing. The coach who recruited him heavily was no longer going to be working at the school he planned to attend, and that meant our son wanted to find a new place to go to school and play ball. *One month* before school started. Not just a new college, but a new place to play baseball in college! Can you feel my stress? If you know anything at all about college sports, you know that was quite the tall order. The idea that our son needed both in such a short time was a tad overwhelming. We started pulling all the strings we could and asking everyone who had been a meaningful part of his athletic career up to that point if they could help.

Our formula for the right school for him had always been academic fit + athletic fit + financial fit = your school, and if you look closely, you'll see some wisdom from Proverbs behind these variables. The right academic fit would keep our son from wasting his time on a degree that lacked the ability to support him and a future family (Proverbs 14:1). The right athletic fit would allow him to grow and develop without being above his ability to play the game (Proverbs 25:6–7). And the correct financial fit would keep him, and us, from incurring a ton of debt just to play a sport (Proverbs 22:26–27).

We were blessed by all the people who offered to help find another college for our son, but some of them brought opportunities that didn't fit the equation. One seemed like an amazing opportunity to play baseball at a Division 2 school that was in the middle of a reorganization and growth effort, but when we looked at the tuition, we were physically sick. My husband and I simply didn't have the money to pay for him to go there. Not only that, but this school didn't offer his chosen field of study. He would have had to pursue a degree that contributed nothing to his desired career plans in order to play there. The school really had to fit all three variables for it to work for us, so with a heaviness in our hearts, we had to tell him no.

I wasn't sure how he was going to take it and prepared myself to stick to my guns, explain why this college couldn't work, and try to convince him to be happy about it. I had all kinds of arguments ready to go, including one that was designed to help him see that the rest of his life—how he would be able to support a family one day—was more important than baseball, but as it turned out, I didn't have to worry. He knew the equation. We had talked about the importance of it many times, not just for us, but for his future. And when he heard about the tuition, combined with the fact that it was so late in the year that there was no athletic scholarship left for him, he knew it wasn't the right option, and he let it go without so much as a gentle disagreement.

That's wisdom for everyday life in action. A practical way of looking at things through the lens of God's Word. We simply held out a standard to him and let it guide our decisions.

Wisdom Calls Out

Proverbs 8:1-4 says, "Doesn't wisdom call out? Doesn't under-standing make her voice heard? At the heights overlooking the road, at the crossroads, she takes her stand. Beside the gates leading into the city, at the main entrance, she cries out." The college formula served as our source of guiding wisdom. It called out to us when we needed it most and made our son's path clear. At the crossroads of the next step in his life, using wisdom as our determining factor helped us know where to go and how to get there. I'm happy to say that God opened the door to another option that was clearly the right one for him. And yes, we man-aged all of this about a month before classes started.

But it could have happened differently.

Sometimes we will hold out the wisdom of God's Word to our children, and just like us, they will be stubborn and refuse to acknowledge or choose it. The key, as we stated above, is that they must want to be wise, and that takes a specific work of God.

Wisdom is literally crying out for our children. Everywhere we go, God's wisdom can be found. But it's not only discover-able, it's actively seeking out those who fear the Lord and take Him seriously. Proverbs 9:4 tells us that wisdom is seeking the inexperienced to show them the way of understanding. This is the good news for our boys.

The bad news is that foolishness does the same thing. Just a few verses later, we learn that folly lacks knowledge and sits by the doorway of her house, calling out to the inexperienced. For the sake of clarity, I want to say that again. *Both* wisdom and folly are calling out to our sons, and to us, but folly's goal isn't to impart wisdom. It's to destroy (Proverbs 9:13–18), so let's look at what can happen when our sons choose *not* to live a life of wisdom. To do that, let's go back to the story of Samson.

Samson might just be the best example of anti-wisdom, or foolishness, that exists in the Bible. We already talked about him a bit a few chapters ago, but I'll refresh your memory. An angel of the Lord, who most biblical scholars think was probably Jesus Himself, came to Samson's parents to announce his birth. Not only did they have the honor of being visited by Jesus, they also had the honor of raising a Nazarite. You may remember that to be a Nazarite meant to be set apart, usually for a specific time, to fulfill a specific plan of the Lord. But in Samson's case, he was to be a Nazarite for his entire life, and this vow didn't just affect Samson after birth. The angel told the couple that Samson's mom also had to abstain from alcohol and any unclean food while she carried him, and they could never cut Samson's hair.

It was a great, clean start to our story. We have every indication that Samson's parents set him up for success, obeying the angel's commands, but somewhere along the way, something went very wrong. The guy we know from Sunday school lessons as the strongest man who ever lived, as Skip Heitzig puts it, "was strong before men; he was weak before women. . . . Though he was a man of faith, he was not a faithful man. . . . He [was] living through his eyeballs."[2] In other words, Samson made decisions based on what he could see in front of him rather than the wisdom that comes from believing God's Word, a step of faith that often requires us to act based on what we can't see. Here are a few of the things he got wrong:

- Hebrew wisdom demanded taking a wife from among his own people (Exodus 34:12–16), but Samson married a Philistine woman who was beautiful to the eyes, but definitely not of Hebrew descent.

- Hebrew wisdom held faithfulness in marriage, and faithfulness to the marriage bed, in high regard (Proverbs 5:15–21), but Samson slept with at least one woman who wasn't his wife.

- The Nazarite vow demanded extreme purity. Nazarites weren't allowed to drink alcohol or even touch grapes. They couldn't touch dead things or cut their hair (Judges 13), but Samson broke that vow multiple times. He walked through a vineyard, touched the carcass of a lion he had killed, and eventually allowed his hair to be cut, leading to his utter downfall.

Samson tried to live out his calling but did so without any sense of the need to stay away from sin or keep himself holy while doing it. He trusted the wrong people, placing his faith in those who only wanted to hurt him (Judges 16). And he was a loner. Samson didn't seek out the counsel of wise people. Instead, he listened to those who meant him harm.

According to Warren Wiersbe, "Samson was unpredictable and undependable because he was double-minded, and 'a double-minded man is unstable in all his ways' (James 1:8)."[3] This is what we *don't* want for our boys—to be double-minded, unstable, and unpredictable. Foolishness, according to Proverbs, can be hard to get rid of, so we must teach our boys to recognize God's wisdom, and then pray that they choose it.

"LORD, LET HIM HEAR WISDOM" PRAYERS

Proverbs 1:7—"The fear of the LORD is the beginning of knowledge; fools despise wisdom and discipline."

PRAYER: Father, help _____ to be a wise man, fearing you. Keep him from being a foolish man who despises wisdom. In Jesus' name, Amen.

Proverbs 1:20–21—"Wisdom calls out in the street; she makes her voice heard in the public squares. She cries out above the commotion; she speaks at the entrance of the city gates."

PRAYER: Lord, open _____'s ears to hear your wisdom calling. Tune his ears to recognize you when you make yourself known. In Jesus' name, Amen.

Proverbs 2:1–8—"My son, if you accept my words and store up my commands within you, listening closely to wisdom and directing your heart to understanding; furthermore, if you call out to insight and lift your voice to understanding, if you seek it like silver and search for it like hidden treasure, then you will understand the fear of the LORD and discover the knowledge of God. For the LORD gives wisdom; from his mouth come knowledge and understanding. He stores up success for the upright; He is a shield for those who live with integrity so that he may guard the paths of justice and protect the way of his faithful followers."

PRAYER: Father, make _____ value your words and commands more than the most precious of treasures. May he seek you for the wisdom he needs, and may you be a shield for him as he walks with integrity, knowledge, and understanding. In Jesus' name, Amen.

Proverbs 3:7—"Don't be wise in your own eyes; fear the LORD and turn away from evil."

PRAYER: Lord, help _____ to see wisdom beyond himself. Don't allow him to think his way is the only way. Instead, lead him to fear you and turn from evil. In Jesus' name, Amen.

Proverbs 4:7—"Wisdom is supreme—so get wisdom. And whatever else you get, get understanding."

PRAYER: Lord, help _____ to see your wisdom and your understanding of the world as the most valuable thing he can possess. In Jesus' name, Amen.

Proverbs 9:1–6—"Wisdom has built her house; she has carved out her seven pillars. She has prepared her meat; she has mixed her wine; she has also set her table. She has sent out her female servants; she calls out from the highest points of the city: 'Whoever is inexperienced, enter here!' To the one who lacks sense, she says, 'Come, eat my bread, and drink the wine I have mixed. Leave inexperience behind, and you will live; pursue the way of understanding.'"

PRAYER: Father, help _____ to hear the voice of wisdom as she calls for him, leaving inexperience behind so he can understand your ways. In Jesus' name, Amen.

Proverbs 17:28—"Even a fool is considered wise when he keeps silent—discerning, when he seals his lips."

PRAYER: Father, give _____ the ability to discern when to keep his mouth shut. In Jesus' name, Amen.

James 3:17—"But the wisdom from above is first pure, then peace-loving, gentle, compliant, full of mercy and good fruits, unwavering, without pretense."

PRAYER: Lord, as _____ searches for the wisdom he needs to live this life, give him wisdom that is pure, peace-loving, gentle, compliant, full of mercy and good fruits, unwavering, and without pretense. In Jesus' name, Amen.

Ephesians 5:15—"Pay careful attention, then, to how you walk—not as unwise people but as wise."

PRAYER: Father, give _____ eyes to see what his life looks like from your perspective, paying careful attention to walk in the wisdom you give. In Jesus' name, Amen.

James 1:5—"Now if any of you lacks wisdom, he should ask God—who gives to all generously and ungrudgingly—and it will be given to him."

PRAYER: Lord, as _____ walks along the path of life, remind him that he can ask you for the wisdom he needs, and when he does, be faithful to give it to him generously and without limits. In Jesus' name, Amen.

PRAYERS AND NOTES

5

LORD, PLACE A GUARD OVER HIS MOUTH

The tension in the gym that evening was palpable. The junior varsity basketball game had been chippy the entire four quarters, and the score reflected two teams who had worked hard, neither of whom wanted to lose.

My son loves basketball, and he isn't usually a player who gets a lot of fouls called against him, but this game was a different story. It had been so physical that toward the end most of the players on both sides of the ball were on the verge of fouling out, and if I remember correctly, at least one of our starters already had.

In a whirlwind last two minutes of the game, the ball was turned over multiple times—first we stole it, then they stole it, then we stole it, then they stole it—back and forth, ball popping out of one team's hands into the other's, creating sheer panic for the fans and players. Somehow, my son was able to take control of the ball and hit the go-ahead basket for our team. The crowd went crazy, and that's when I noticed it happening.

My younger son smiles a lot. For years, people have commented on his big smile, especially when things aren't going well for him. When he was younger, maybe around ten, he started pitching for his travel baseball team. When he pitched well, he smiled. When he didn't pitch well, he smiled. People around me would say, "Look at the pitcher! He just got a terrible call from the umpire and he's still smiling!" It was fun to hear them compliment him, but the truth is that I knew something they didn't about the young man on the mound. He has different kinds of smiles, and the one they were seeing wasn't a happy smile. It was a "I'm going to smile to keep from completely losing it" kind of smile.

That's the smile I saw come out in the last few seconds of the game that day, and it made me watch him more closely. Zoomed in now, I could see that the guy from the other team was all over him defensively, and not only that, but there was a lot of smack talk happening. Mostly, my son was taking it and playing his game, but when that smile came out, I knew we had a potential problem.

In the last few seconds of the game, his teammate sealed the deal with another basket and we won, and I watched as the opposing team came unglued. Apparently, that was all my son could take. He took a few steps toward the player who had been guarding him and started yelling back at him.

I couldn't hear the words he was saying, but I knew it wasn't going to help the situation, so I yelled, "SHUT YOUR MOUTH!" He heard me, but didn't stop, so I yelled it again, a bit louder this time: "SHUT YOUR MOUTH!" He looked at me, threw his arms out exasperated, and walked away. Thankfully, our coach saw clearly what was happening (not just with my son—both teams were on the verge of imploding) and began aggressively herding our team off the court to the locker room. Crisis averted. (For the record, I don't advocate for yelling at your child while he's on the court. This game was on the verge of a major brawl, so it felt right, but I hadn't done it before, and haven't done it since.)

After he got home late that night, I asked my son to explain what happened during the game that made him react to the other player in a way that he rarely does. He said, "Mom, that guy was mouthing off at me the entire game. He never stopped. I tried to ignore him, but when we won he said some bad stuff and I just lost it. I didn't mean to, but I wasn't going to let him talk to me or my team that way."

What in the world is a mama to do with that information?

Navigating the sports world, where there is so much competition, aggression, and opportunity to lose it in the heat of the moment has been one of the hardest things we've had to handle as our boys grew up. How do you act like a Christian in a world where it's normal to put other people down, talk smack, and make it your goal to take another person's spot? How do you stay good friends with someone and point them to Christ when your goal is to sit your best friend on the bench so you can play instead? And while sports has been our main exposure to this, I've learned that the issues go beyond it. A teacher told me, "I've been a teacher for twenty years, and we are definitely dealing with more unkind, mean, hurtful words and actions than ever before! So many responses are 'I was just playing.' Our counselors are overwhelmed and at a loss for how to handle all of it."

But it isn't happening only in the public school arena. Another teacher said, "The way they talk to one another breaks my heart. I see it in our Bible classes. My son is a gamer, and there is a lot of that in the gaming world too." A mom in one of my boymom groups said, "I feel like this is an issue with teens and adults. The respect and consideration for other people's feelings and opinions seems to have gotten lost in our society over the last several years."

Yes. This.

From a scientific perspective, our children's brains aren't fully developed until they're twenty-four or twenty-five years old. The part of the brain that handles emotions and decision-making skills isn't fully developed until well beyond their teenage years. On top of that, it's the rare teenage boy who has a well-developed, mature Christian faith to guide and restrain his personality. Have I mentioned that at this age testosterone is coursing through their veins at higher rates than it may ever again? So we're talking about an age where the spiritual, physical, and emotional development of our sons is messy at best, a volcanic eruption waiting to happen at worst. It's no wonder they need their mamas' prayers to cover them when they aren't quite equipped to cover themselves.

I've prayed Psalm 141:3 for myself and my children for as long as I can remember. It says, "Set a guard, O Lord, over my mouth; keep watch over the door of my lips!" (ESV). Since the advent of social media, the guard of Psalm 141 seems to have slipped off the faces of most Christians entirely—certainly of the culture at large—along with the awareness that it even needs to be there. And while there is a lot of good that can come from social media, the bad is that it has made us a careless, unfiltered people, less considerate of other people's feelings and more inclined to put other people in their place—from behind the safety of the computer monitor or phone—when we disagree with them. I submit to you that this phenomenon, combined with the unprecedented access our children have to insider views of celebrity personal lives, may, at least in part, be responsible for the put-down culture we live in.

I'm not going to spend any time in this chapter providing solutions for the sports world. I don't have them, and frankly, we're still in it, trying to figure it out for ourselves and our sons as we go. We haven't been perfect at it, and we aren't on the other side of it, so I'll reserve that chapter for another book and another time when I have more experience. For now, I want to talk about the power of words and why it's so important for us to teach our sons to control theirs. Perhaps that study alone can help us navigate the world our children are growing up in.

The Power of the Tongue

I sat at the breakfast table with my son and read over twenty verses from the Bible out loud, one right after the other, on the power of our words. There are hundreds of verses across both the Old and New Testaments that either speak directly about or allude to the idea that our words have power. My friend and pastor Ward Harris said, "When God says something once, we should pay attention. But when He says it over and over again, we *have* to let it impact the way we live."[1] That morning, when I had finished reading, as he quietly ate his bagel with cream cheese, my son looked at me and said, "I get it, Mom. It's important." Yes, son, it is.

James spends one entire chapter talking about the power of the tongue. He opens chapter three by reminding his readers that not everyone should be teachers, because they are held to the strictest standards. Then he launches into ten straight verses that describe what an untamed tongue can do. I'd like to share those in *The Message* version:

> A bit in the mouth of a horse controls the whole horse. A small rudder on a huge ship in the hands of a skilled captain sets a course in the face of the strongest winds. A word out of your mouth may seem of no account, but it can accomplish nearly anything—or destroy it!
>
> It only takes a spark, remember, to set off a forest fire. A careless or wrongly placed word out of your mouth can do that.

By our speech we can ruin the world, turn harmony to chaos, throw mud on a reputation, send the whole world up in smoke and go up in smoke with it, smoke right from the pit of hell.

This is scary: You can tame a tiger, but you can't tame a tongue —it's never been done. The tongue runs wild, a wanton killer. With our tongues we bless God our Father; with the same tongues we curse the very men and women he made in his image. Curses and blessings out of the same mouth!

My friends, this can't go on. A spring doesn't gush fresh water one day and brackish the next, does it? Apple trees don't bear strawberries, do they? Raspberry bushes don't bear apples, do they? You're not going to dip into a polluted mud hole and get a cup of clear, cool water, are you?

vv. 3–12

Having the ability to speak is a good thing—a God-given thing. After all, communication is how we share the gospel, sing, pray, and praise God. Not having the gift of speech doesn't make these things impossible, but it certainly makes them harder. Words are good, and God gave them to us to point to Him, and to give life to others, but at the same time, words can be some of the most hurtful things we ever experience. The old adage "Sticks and stones may break my bones, but words will never hurt me" is *wrong*. It's a straight-up lie. How many of us, when asked, could immediately remember words that were spoken to us that have defined much of the way we think about ourselves, changed relationships forever, or caused us to doubt God's assignment for us? I can. And it isn't just the words themselves that are the problem.

My husband and I get along well, but if we have an argument of some kind, 99 percent of the time it's because of the *way* we said something, not *what* we said in and of itself. The results of a popular study on how we understand the spoken word might shock you. In the complete package of what is said and understood at any given time, tone of voice accounts for 38 percent of the overall message, 55 percent of the overall message is communicated through body language, and only 7 percent of the overall message—its literal meaning—is communicated through choice of words.[2]

Consider the implications of that for how our children communicate most of the time! Social media is ripe with opportunities for our children to be misunderstood, and because everything can be screen recorded, the chances of them getting caught and suffering major consequences for their choices are much higher than when you and I were the same age. It's a hard world out there to be a teenager in right now, so we have to do our best to teach them to be men who submit their hearts to God, allow Him to lead them, and make things right when they go wrong.

Out of the Abundance of the Heart

Another verse I have quoted often to my children over the years (so often that they may or may not groan when they hear it) is Luke 6:45. In the ESV, it says, "The good person out of the good treasure of his heart produces good, and the evil person out of his evil treasure produces evil, *for out of the abundance of the heart his mouth speaks*" (emphasis mine). Out of the abundance of the heart the mouth speaks. It's one of those really true truths that proves itself in a human life over and over again as we react to what's happening around us. Maybe you've heard this illustration before: If I'm holding a cup of water and someone bumps up against me, causing me to lose my grip on the cup, what will be all over the floor? Answer? Water. Right, but why is there water on the floor? The common answer when I pose this question is that there's water on the floor because someone knocked the cup out of my hand, but that's the wrong answer. The correct answer is that there's water on the floor because there was water in the cup. If the cup had been empty, there would be no water on the floor.

It's the same with our hearts. When life comes along and knocks us, either in big or small ways, what's in our hearts will come out.

The reason I've bored my children to tears with the truth of Luke 6:45 is that I want it to stick with them. Even if they roll their eyes at it now, one day, I pray it will take root and grow, and they'll be men who choose to consider what resides in their hearts as very important. I hope they'll keep short accounts with God, confessing their sin and dealing with things like bitterness, unforgiveness, or pride, so that when they're pressed (and they will be), good things come out. I want them to be the kind of men God can speak to and correct. When they hear His voice clearly, I pray they'll repent and get cleaned up on the inside. This is how they'll learn to tame their tongues. I can't think of a more perfect example of this in the New Testament than Zacchaeus.

Zacchaeus's story is found in the book of Luke. He was short ("Zacchaeus was a wee little man . . ." Remember the song?), and he was dirty. Not physically dirty, metaphorically. Zacchaeus was a tax collector. His name means "righteous one,"[3] but he was anything but righteous in his dealings with the people he took care of. He overcharged them and worked for the Gentiles. Zacchaeus had gotten rich off dirty business and only worried about his own glory and provision, and the people hated him for it.

And then he met Jesus.

Listen to his story in Luke 19:

There was a man named Zacchaeus who was a chief tax collector, and he was rich. He was trying to see who Jesus was, but he was not able because of the crowd, since he was a short man. So running ahead, he climbed up a sycamore tree to see Jesus, since he was about to pass that way.

vv. 2–4

We aren't told why Zacchaeus wanted to see Jesus so badly. Maybe it was just that he was famous, or maybe God had already been working in his heart to prepare him for the moment when Jesus would pass his way. Whatever the case, his encounter with Jesus changed everything.

When Jesus came to the place, he looked up and said to him, "Zacchaeus, hurry and come down because today it is necessary for me to stay at your house." . . . Zacchaeus stood there and said to the Lord, "Look, I'll give half of my possessions to the poor, Lord. And if I have extorted anything from anyone, I'll pay back four times as much."

vv. 5, 8

One issue for many boys is that to stay quiet, be humble, or be kind to those who are unkind is considered uncool and unmanly. It's part of the reason my son stood up to the other basketball player that day after the game. He was being mistreated and felt that staying quiet allowed the mistreatment of his team members. Boys today (boys for all time?) feel that to be meek, as Jesus was meek, to love those who curse them, or simply not to retaliate or defend themselves is a sign of weakness. It makes them feel small when they want to feel big.

Of course, there were times when Jesus got angry, but I've yet to see a young boy whose anger was as pure and righteous as that of Jesus. It isn't wrong to stand up for others, but in general, this refusal to stand down is a worldly measurement of a man, and one that is incredibly hard to battle. In the case of Zacchaeus, we see the opposite play out—a small man becoming big. There wasn't anything he could do to make himself physically bigger, but as Zacchaeus humbled himself and trusted Jesus, his countenance and character got bigger, and that's the true measure of a man. Suddenly, as Zacchaeus gave back what wasn't rightfully his, he was the biggest man around.

This is the kind of response we want our boys to have when what's in their hearts reveals itself to be dirty. Repentance and an effort to make things right. Zacchaeus didn't just say, "I'll turn and follow Jesus." He didn't just acknowledge that he had done something wrong. He made the wrong right.

One of our sons got in trouble at school recently for saying something unkind about one of his teammates, and while I'm glad his coach held him accountable for his words, they were fairly benign. It could've been a lot worse than it was, but part of the consequence of his actions was that he had to go make it right with the boy on his team. He had to humble himself and say he was sorry for saying something that hurt him. Some might say it was overkill, or nitpicky . . . boys will be boys . . . but I'm glad it happened. It set a standard for our son that I hope he'll rise to in the coming days. The ability to lay down their own glory for the sake of the glory of God is something many men (and women) struggle deeply with. The world needs more men who have won a hard-fought victory over sin, so let's not take that battle from them. Instead, let's help them to be accountable for what comes out of their hearts, understand how their words make others feel, and respect the power of their words.

"LORD, PLACE A GUARD OVER HIS MOUTH" PRAYERS

First Peter 3:10—"For the one who wants to love life and to see good days, let him keep his tongue from evil and his lips from speaking deceit."

> **PRAYER:** Father, give _____ the desire to please you with the words that come out of his mouth, and as he does, bless him with life and good days. In Jesus' name, Amen.

Ephesians 4:29—"No foul language should come from your mouth, but only what is good for building up someone in need, so that it gives grace to those who hear."

> **PRAYER:** Lord, inspire _____ to use his words for good, to build up those around him and give grace to those who hear. In Jesus' name, Amen.

Proverbs 15:4—"The tongue that heals is a tree of life, but a devious tongue breaks the spirit."

> **PRAYER:** Lord, let _____ have the desire to use his tongue to give life, and not break the spirit of others. In Jesus' name, Amen.

Matthew 15:11—"It's not what goes into the mouth that defiles a person, but what comes out of the mouth—this defiles a person."

> **PRAYER:** Father, help _____ to pay attention to what's in his heart. When he sees bitterness, anger, jealousy, or other things that don't please you, give him the desire to make it right so that he might not be defiled. In Jesus' name, Amen.

Proverbs 21:23—"The one who guards his mouth and tongue keeps himself out of trouble."

PRAYER: Lord, help _____ to see the need to guard his mouth and tongue so that he stays out of unnecessary trouble. In Jesus' name, Amen.

Psalm 34:13—"Keep your tongue from evil and your lips from deceitful speech."

PRAYER: Lord, help _____ to recognize when the words he's about to speak are evil or deceitful, and enable him to keep them to himself. In Jesus' name, Amen.

Psalm 141:3—"Lord, set up a guard for my mouth; keep watch at the door of my lips."

PRAYER: Father, when _____ is unable to close his mouth, or choose wise, life-giving words, please do it for him. Make him unable to speak when his words don't please you. In Jesus' name, Amen.

Proverbs 17:27—"The one who has knowledge restrains his words, and one who keeps a cool head is a person of understanding."

PRAYER: Lord, build _____ knowledge so that he has the power to restrain his words. Give him the ability to keep a cool head in difficult circumstances. In Jesus' name, Amen.

Proverbs 12:18–19—"There is one who speaks rashly, like a piercing sword; but the tongue of the wise brings healing. Truthful lips endure forever, but a lying tongue, only a moment."

PRAYER: Father, inspire _____ to use his tongue for healing. Help him to see how painful his words can be when he uses them to pierce others. In Jesus' name, Amen.

Proverbs 15:1–2—"A gentle answer turns away anger, but a harsh word stirs up wrath. The tongue of the wise makes knowledge attractive, but the mouth of fools blurts out foolishness."

PRAYER: Lord, may _____ have the ability to be gentle with his responses. Help him think before he speaks, making the knowledge he has of you and your ways attractive to those around him. In Jesus' name, Amen.

PRAYERS AND NOTES

6

LORD, HELP HIM STAND

They crept carefully and quietly across the carpeted floor of the bedroom, blankets tied around their necks like superhero capes, until they got to the doorframe, and came to a complete stop. Slowly, my rambunctious boys peeked their heads around the corner, hoping to catch a glimpse of their adversary, their mortal enemy—sin.

But the supervillain they expected to see wasn't there. In fact, nothing at all lurked behind the door waiting to pounce on them, and they were a little disappointed. Deflated even. There would be no fierce battle of the ages today, and I could see the question in their eyes as they turned to look at me still sitting on the far side of the room where we'd just had a Bible study lesson on Cain and Abel. Where, they wondered, was this crouching foe that desired to harm them, harm their family?

I laughed, overjoyed and emotional about how seriously they took the words of Genesis 4:7, as God says to Cain, "If you do what is right, won't you be accepted? But if you do not do what is right, sin is crouching at the door. Its desire is for you, but you must rule over it." To my little boys, then around five and seven, those were fighting words. In a season where everything was an epic battle of good versus evil, the idea that there was something crouching behind the door ready to do them harm was cause for alarm.

They expected to see a real foe on the other side of the door that day, but the fact that they didn't created an excellent opportunity for me to talk to them about how the enemy works. He doesn't, I told them, have horns or dress in red. There's no tail either. If he did show up in person, it's much more likely that he would look just like you and me (minus your capes). He'd be very handsome, with an attractive personality that drew you to him in an almost unexplainable way. There would be an edge to him too, that caused you to feel a bit of caution, and his words would be as smooth as honey, making you wonder if what you thought was true really was. "Did God really say . . ." (Genesis 3:1) would drip from his mouth, and you'd find yourself wondering if He really did.

The enemy, I told them, comes disguised as an angel of light (2 Corinthians 11:14–15), in some cases appearing to be a servant of righteousness. This is why we must learn to tell the difference between right and wrong, and the only way we can do that, I said, is by knowing God's Word. It is our guide to rule over this crafty, sneaky foe whose only job is to kill, steal, and destroy (John 10:10).

It was a memorable day for me. It isn't every day that we're given such an easy-to-demonstrate biblical truth that captures the imagination of our children, coming alive for them in a profound way. The story of Cain's battle with sin spoke the language of their little boy hearts, and I hoped it would stick with them even as they grew too old to wear blankets tied around their necks as capes. Imagine my delight when I asked my children, then fifteen and seventeen years old, to tell me what the enemy's job was. To hear them both say, "He comes only to kill, steal, and destroy" lit me up on the inside, and when I asked if he was their friend, they firmly said no. Then, I hesitantly asked them to tell me what sin does, hoping against hope they would remember the day they prepared themselves to fight for my honor in their upstairs bedroom. It was my younger son who said, "Sin is crouching at the door . . ." and then my older chimed in with him, memory jogged, "Its desire is for you, but you must rule over it."

When I first heard the story of Cain and Abel as a young child in Sunday school, it seemed a bit unfair to me that Cain's sacrifice wasn't good enough for God. I didn't understand, at least at first, that there was really nothing wrong with Cain's gift itself. The problem rested squarely in Cain's heart. Cain wasn't right with God. Abel was, and so God spoke the words of Genesis 4:7 to Cain, giving him a warning about the power sin could have over him if he didn't fix his heart problem. Sadly, Cain didn't fix it, and sin's desire for him won the day when he murdered his brother, Abel.

All of us have the capacity to sin. We are prone to sin because we are sinners, and the sin that lives in each of us is happy to lie in wait until the perfect time, resting comfortably until it can spring into action. It crouches right around the corner, watching for the right opportunity to take us over, and when sin is awakened this way, it can grow into something murderous, much like it did in Cain.

The good news is that Christ also stands at the door and knocks (Revelation 3:20). Wisdom cries out in the street, accessible to all who listen to her (Proverbs 1:20). Our boys will have to choose whose voice they open their heart to, and it's our job to pray that when they're faced with the temptation to sin, they'll stand.

Rooted and Grounded

When I was about twelve, Hurricane Hugo, a powerful category five hurricane, hit the mountains of southwestern Virginia, where I lived with my family. Normally, our mountains protect us from severe hurricane damage, but with Hugo, they did not. At least not fully. The damage Hugo inflicted actually caused the name *Hugo* to be retired from among eligible Atlantic hurricane names. Sixty-seven people were killed, and the storm caused over $11 billion in damage, more than any other hurricane preceding it. We lived several hours inland from the East Coast, where Hugo did the most damage, but the impact of the storm was still enough that we got out of school for a couple of days. I spent the night with one of my best friends, Michelle, and had a blast. Meanwhile, my parents were losing trees around our house; they fell under the force of the wind, ripping roots right out of the ground. Trees falling is the number one memory people in my area have about Hurricane Hugo.

My parents live on the fringes of a forest. Their land spans about five acres of mostly wooded mountainside, so there was some concern about trees falling on the house. In fact, some of the trees on the hill behind my childhood home eventually had to be taken down before they fell because Hugo unsettled them. Storms will do that when trees aren't deeply rooted or secure, or are old and dying, which is what happened in my mom and dad's front and back yard. The trees that fell were old, some of them already dying, and their roots had shriveled. When the winds of Hugo came against them, they simply couldn't hold their ground.

This is exactly what we don't want to happen to our boys. But what does it take for a person to be rooted and grounded? Consider Psalm 1:1–3 (ESV):

Blessed is the man who walks not in the counsel of the wicked, nor stands in the way of sinners, nor sits in the seat of scoffers; but his delight is in the law of the LORD, and on his law he meditates day and night. He is like a tree planted by streams of water that yields its fruit in its season, and its leaf does not wither. In all that he does, he prospers.

Tony Evans defines a blessing as "the God-given capacity to experience, enjoy, and extend the goodness and favor of God in your life."[1] On the contrary, a worldly definition of being blessed looks like having the material things you want, plus having health, wealth, obedient and healthy children, and a happy marriage. This passage teaches us that the man (or woman) who is truly blessed by God, who delights in God's law and in God Himself, will be securely grounded, able to thrive and survive because he's getting the nutrients and provision he needs.

Interestingly, the psalmist here takes the time to demonstrate how to get securely grounded and blessed by God by telling us what not to do instead of telling us what to do. For our sons to be planted in such a way that allows their roots to grow deep, stabilizing them when the winds blow and the rains come, they must not listen to the counsel of wicked people, hang around with sinners, or sit with people who mock the things of God. This is a stern warning for our boys if they want to be able to stand when the storm of the enemy comes for them. Being blessed by God, living a prosperous life that honors God and doesn't give the enemy a foothold or an easy in, requires being rooted and grounded in truth.

Growing in their Christian walk in a way that allows them to take a stand requires our boys to keep putting their faith in Christ (Colossians 2:6–7). Not just the one time at salvation, but day after day after day . . . moment by moment walking with Him, applying His truth to their lives, and not giving influence to things and people who could lead them astray. Matthew Henry says, "The great concern of those who have received Christ is *to walk in Him*—to make their practices conformable to their principles."[2] In my experience, this takes time and maturity to do well, but then that's the point, isn't it? Trees start as a seed and grow over many years into maturity. They can't stand tall, lending us their shade and protection, when they're little. They have to have life poured into them by the sun and rain so their roots can grow strong and deep. Only then will they be able to withstand the storms.

Stand Firm

In my book *Everyday Prayers for Patience,* I tell the story about when God showed me something significant about how I was praying for my boys. One evening, I snuck into their rooms after they were already asleep, laid my hands on them, and began to pray. In that sweet moment, I got overwhelmed with their innocence and started to pray for God to keep them from evil. It just felt like too much to think about them being harmed by their enemy when they looked so sweet and young in their beds. I shared that story with my women's Bible study the next morning and was gifted a significant piece of wisdom from one of the older moms in my group. She said, "You're praying for the wrong thing, Brooke. They are going to see and experience evil in this world. . . . They are going to be tempted. Your prayer needs to be that when they encounter evil, when they are tempted, they'll stand firm."[3]

In 1 Peter 5:8–9, we find the road map to standing firm: "Be sober-minded, be alert. Your adversary the devil is prowling around like a roaring lion, looking for anyone he can devour. Resist him, firm in the faith."

Matthew Henry says of the devil, "He is . . . hungry, fierce, strong, and cruel, the fierce and greedy pursuer of souls. . . . His whole design is to devour and destroy souls."[4] And so to withstand him—to stay ahead of him—we must do these things:

- Be sober
- Be vigilant
- Be watchful

Be Sober

I stood in the basement of my childhood home, in front of the washer and dryer, with my dad and my then boyfriend (now husband) on either side. My laundry was sopping wet, freshly moved from one machine to the other, and I was attempting to hurriedly throw them as such from the dryer to a laundry basket when these two men of my life intervened.

The simple story is that I had come home from grad school for the weekend to visit, started a load of laundry late in the day on Sunday, and then realized that I had left some of the items I needed to get the rest of my schoolwork done in Lynchburg, where I was in school. I had assignments due on Tuesday, and when I realized that I couldn't possibly get them done according to my previously planned work schedule, I panicked and started throwing wet laundry in a basket with the intention of making the 2.5-hour trip back to campus late at night. Both of these men who loved me knew me well enough to know that it wasn't a good idea for me to drive in a panic. I distinctly remember my dad looking me in the eye and telling me to get a grip on myself. Actually, his exact words were "Brooke, this is mind over matter. Tell yourself how to feel."

To be sober means to be able to govern the outer and inner man, and I was not doing a good job of it that day. I wasn't drunk, or physically unable to control myself, but I wasn't *choosing* to control myself in the face of a stressful situation. I had a habit (reputation?) of being a reactor, and my dad knew it. I often allowed my emotions to run amuck first, and then had cleanup to do afterward. He also knew that he needed to help me calm down before getting behind the wheel of a car.

Thankfully, the Lord has worked on me in this area faithfully. I can still feel the initial surge of emotions when something happens outside of my control. But I'm now much better able to control my reaction to it, in part because my dad brought it to my attention and started the process of teaching me how. When he said to me in the basement, "This is mind over matter," he was saying, "Be sober-minded, control your thoughts and you'll control your emotions." This, to me, translates perfectly to Philippians 4:8, which says, "Finally brothers and sisters, whatever is true, whatever is honorable, whatever is just, whatever is pure, whatever is lovely, whatever is commendable—if there is any moral excellence and if there is anything praiseworthy—dwell on these things." I was dwelling on what I couldn't control. My dad helped me switch gears and dwell on something else.

In order to resist their enemy, our sons are going to need us to help them control their inner and outer man, pointing out weaknesses and shortsightedness that could cause them to "wreck the car" if they get behind the wheel when they're out of control. I'm not advocating for being a nagging mom here. But I am saying that no one knows your sons better than you do, so you are uniquely positioned to see the character flaws that might trip them up, lovingly point them out, and help them take steps to master them. And while complete mastery of these shortcomings is ultimately the work of the Holy Spirit in the hearts of our sons, we can begin the process of helping them learn to be sober-minded.

Be Vigilant

When I was learning to drive, the only car that was available to get me from point A to point B was a manual transmission. It was a doozy of one too. My dad bought a light blue Volkswagen Rabbit that needed a new transmission. It was originally an automatic, but the only transmission he could find to replace it was a manual. That meant there was a third pedal on the floor where there had only been two before and we now had to coordinate that pedal, the clutch, with shifting through the gears. It was a fun little car, but because of its unusual circumstances, hard to drive. The clutch was very hard to push in, and you had to have serious upper body strength to change the gears. I've often said that if you could drive that car, you could drive *any* car.

Because of the fun I had with a stick shift, I wanted both of our sons to learn to drive them too. My husband also had one in his first car, and we agreed that it could be a valuable learning experience. Being able to do it made us both feel like we had more control over the car, and that we were in tune with how it felt . . . if a car can feel. We also thought having to drive with both feet and both hands increased the chances that our children would leave their phones alone while driving (at least we hoped)!

We weren't able to get one for our older son, but when it came time to buy a used car for our second, my husband succeeded. After looking for at least two years, he found a small black sedan that had a manual transmission, and the lessons began. I taught the first lesson in the wide-open high school parking lot . . . the same place where I had had my first lesson many years before. We worked on pulling out in first gear and backing up for over an hour before I let him drive around the entire parking lot.

When we got to the back of the school, I shouted, "Watch out! There's a car backing up and it's going to hit you!" The parking lot was empty, but I caught him off guard because I wanted to see how he would react. Would he remember to put the clutch in with the brake? Or would we bounce along until the engine died? I also wanted to demonstrate to him how important it is to be vigilant, especially in a car he's unfamiliar with, with a system he hasn't mastered. Cars do back out of spaces quickly in that parking lot, and there really might be times when he would have to stop suddenly. Carelessness, lack of attention to detail, and being unaware of the situation he was in could be a recipe for disaster, and he needed to remember it.

In the same way, our boys need to remember the danger that is actively seeking to destroy them. We've already established that they have a very real enemy, and that that enemy is on a mission to devour and destroy. "To this end he is unwearied and restless in his malicious endeavors; for he always, night and day, goes about studying and contriving whom he may ensnare to their eternal ruin."[5] Just as our son needed to be prepared for what could happen (even if it couldn't actually happen that particular night) in the high school parking lot, our sons need to be prepared for the enemy's schemes. "God does not make his children carefree in order that they be careless."[6] Carelessness breeds disaster. We have to teach our sons to pay attention and pray for God to help them be alert.

Be Watchful

While being vigilant means to be aware that something *can* happen, being watchful has a preemptive tone to it that moves the believer into a position to prevent the plans of the enemy altogether. Of course, we can pray for God to keep our sons from temptation. But as the wiser mom I told you about earlier in this chapter said, they *will* face temptations. It's inevitable. Our job is not to try to keep them from experiencing them (after all, they learn from failure as much as success), but to teach them how to respond to temptations when they come.

We are a baseball family, and in the game of baseball, it's important to think ahead. Before the next batter steps into the batter's box, my husband taught our kids to be asking themselves, *What is the right thing to do if the ball comes to me in this situation?* For years at the dinner table, our conversations sounded like this:

> You've got a man on first, a man on third, and two outs. You're playing second base. If the ball comes to you, where are you throwing it?

> You're playing shortstop with a man on first and one out. What's your play if the ball comes straight to you?

> The bases are loaded, you're pitching, and it's a full count with two outs. What kind of pitch are you throwing?

The idea here is to teach players to think a play ahead. What will you do if (fill in the blank) happens? When our older son was in the eighth grade, my husband and I sat on a hill above the baseball field in beautiful Bath County, Virginia, and spontaneously wrote a silly poem that illustrates this point. It says:

> May your bat hit the ball,
> May your glove be true,
> Always think one play ahead of you.
> Keep your faith strong,
> Be respectful of Blue,
> If there's one on and one out, be brave and turn two.
> May your hands be quick,

Your throws sure,
And always remember to keep your heart pure.

I designed a print with the poem on it entitled "A Baseball Prayer" for him when he left to play baseball in North Carolina after his senior year of high school, and he's kept it framed on his desk as a reminder ever since.

Always think one play ahead of you. *What will you do if this happens? What will your reaction be if that happens? How will you protect yourself against these circumstances? What decisions will you make now to ensure you're never in this situation?* These are the kinds of questions we can teach our sons to ask themselves so that when those things happen, and they will, they'll know where they're throwing the ball, so to speak.

Thankfully, the Bible doesn't leave us high and dry here. We have specific instructions on how to avoid evil. The beginning of 1 Corinthians 6:18 says, "Flee sexual immorality!" but I think this principle applies to all sin. The Bible doesn't tell us to dance as close as possible to the line that separates sinning from not sinning. It tells us to turn around and run in the opposite direction.

"LORD, HELP HIM STAND" PRAYERS

Ephesians 6:13–14—"For this reason take up the full armor of God, so that you may be able to resist in the evil day, and having prepared everything, to take your stand. Stand, therefore, with truth like a belt around your waist, righteousness like armor on your chest."

PRAYER: Lord, dress _____ in your armor today, that he might be able to resist in the evil day, and take his stand against the enemy. In Jesus' name, Amen.

First Peter 5:8–9—"Be sober-minded, be alert. Your adversary the devil is prowling around like a roaring lion, looking for anyone he can devour. Resist him, firm in the faith."

> **PRAYER:** Father, help _____ to be sober-minded and alert to the schemes of the devil. Give him the power to resist, standing firm in his faith. In Jesus' name, Amen.

First Corinthians 16:13—"Be alert, stand firm in the faith, be courageous, be strong."

> **PRAYER:** Lord, make _____ alert and firm in his faith. Fill him with courage and strength. In Jesus' name, Amen.

Psalm 1:1–3—"How happy is the one who does not walk in the advice of the wicked or stand in the pathway with sinners or sit in the company of mockers! Instead, his delight is in the LORD's instruction, and he meditates on it day and night. He is like a tree planted beside flowing streams that bears its fruit in its season, and its leaf does not wither. Whatever he does prospers."

> **PRAYER:** Lord, help _____ to discern the hearts of the people he allows to influence his life, staying away from the advice of the wicked, not standing in the pathway with sinners, and not sitting in the company of mockers. Plant him instead by streams of flowing water, giving him the nourishment he needs to prosper in you. In Jesus' name, Amen.

Colossians 2:6–7—"So then, just as you have received Christ Jesus as Lord, continue to walk in him, being rooted and built up in him and established in the faith, just as you were taught, and overflowing with gratitude."

> **PRAYER:** Father, I believe you have started a good work in
> _____. Please continue to guide him toward you over
> and over again, and woo him so that he desires to walk with
> you. Establish his faith and build him into a man you can use.
> In Jesus' name, Amen.

Colossians 3:12–14—"Therefore, as God's chosen ones, holy
and dearly loved, put on compassion, kindness, humility,
gentleness, and patience, bearing with one another and for-
giving one another if anyone has a grievance against another.
Just as the Lord has forgiven you, so you are also to forgive.
Above all, put on love, which is the perfect bond of unity."

> **PRAYER:** Lord, make my son a man of compassion, showing kind-
> ness, gentleness, patience, and forgiveness to those he walks
> with in this life. Help him to see how much he's been forgiven
> in you so that he can freely extend that forgiveness to those
> around him. In Jesus' name, Amen.

Ephesians 3:16–18—"I pray . . . that Christ may dwell in
your hearts through faith. I pray that you, being rooted and
firmly established in love, may be able to comprehend with
all the saints what is the length and width, height and depth
of God's love."

> **PRAYER:** Father, root and ground _____ in your love.
> Make him able to comprehend with the saints how long, wide,
> high, and deep it is so that he overflows with love toward other
> people. In Jesus' name, Amen.

John 15:5—"I am the vine; you are the branches. The one
who remains in me and I in him produces much fruit, because you can do nothing without me."

PRAYER: Lord, keep _____ connected to you. May he remain in you and you in him so that his life can produce much fruit. In Jesus' name, Amen.

Matthew 13:6—"But when the sun came up, it was scorched, and since it had no root, it withered away."

PRAYER: Lord, give _____ deep roots in his knowledge of and faith in you. Use the circumstances of his life to draw him closer to you and increase his faith. In Jesus' name, Amen.

First Samuel 17:45—"David said to the Philistine, 'You come against me with a sword, spear, and javelin, but I come against you in the name of the LORD of Armies, the God of the ranks of Israel—you have defied him.'"

PRAYER: Lord, give _____ a passion for your name and your honor. Make him a man who will step up against the odds to defend you and the things that matter for your kingdom. In Jesus' name, Amen.

PRAYERS AND NOTES

7

LORD, OPEN HIS EYES

If our prayer for ourselves is "Lord, show me," a powerful prayer for our sons is "Lord, show *him.*"

I was asked in an interview to share the place in my life where I have most grappled with patience. Patience, as I understand it, is a fruit of the Spirit. Along with love, joy, peace, kindness, goodness, faithfulness, gentleness, and self-control, patience is not a feeling; it's a fruit. Galatians 5 tells us that the believer in Jesus gets a seed of all these character traits planted in them when they come to Christ. That means we already have a seed of patience, or any of the other fruit of the Spirit, living in us right now. And if they're already in us, and if they're fruit, they can be grown. With love, attention, and the choice to prune and nurture these fruits, they can grow stronger. Hope is not listed in the Scriptures specifically as a fruit of the Spirit. But I can be patient because God has already planted patience in me, and that fills me with hope.

That said, I have probably always struggled with patience. My mom's nickname for me is Bee-in-the-bonnet-Boo. My brother called me Brookie-Boo when I was a baby, and it stuck.

My grandmother had nicknames for all nine of her grand-children, and mine became Boo. I'm the baby of the family, and several of my older cousins still call me that. I don't mind a bit, but I won't answer to Bee-in-the-bonnet-Boo. What my mom means by this is that once I get "stung" by a desire for something, I'll keep buzzing around until I can figure out a way to get it. In other words, I struggle to be patient and wait for things . . . all things. But the answer to the direct question I was asked in the interview is that the thing I struggle with most right now is being patient with my teenagers—and with God—as they grow in their maturity in Christ.

Both of my children have made a profession of faith, and as I watch them grow and mature, there are things they embrace that I don't agree with. I don't want to paint a bad picture of them for you . . . both of my kids are walking with the Lord the best way they know how, but sometimes, often, I'm impatient for them to know Jesus the way I do after a lifetime of walking with Him.

The other day, I was talking to one of my children about an expression of my faith I've embraced that some other believers don't. It isn't a matter of sin, but of the freedom we have in Christ to do things differently as believers depending on what God calls *us* to do. This is an area where I feel personally convicted to act a certain way. My son does not yet feel convicted in the same way.

We've had conversations where we've looked at the Word together over this matter. I've explained to him that my position is not one of "You're sinning if you do or don't do this," but one of personal conviction that the Lord has called *me* to live this way. I wish with all my heart that he would choose the same way—and I pray for it—but I have to wait for God to get him there, to mature and develop his faith and *show him* how He wants him to live. I need to have patience and wait for God to open his eyes, and that can be very hard.

But of course, there are other kinds of eye-opening experiences we can pray for our sons to have as they go through life too. Before we can pray for God to mature them in their faith, we have to pray for them to see that there is a God and see their need for a Savior. Once they've given their lives to Him, we can pray for them to see the world through God's eyes instead of their own, and to see the needs of others.

Open the Eyes of His Understanding

In Romans 1:18–20, we read these words:

> For God's wrath is revealed from heaven against all godlessness and unrighteousness of people who by their unrighteousness suppress the truth, since what can be known about God is evident among them, because God has shown it to them. For his invisible attributes, that is, his eternal power and divine nature, have been clearly seen since the creation of the world, being understood through what he has made. As a result, people are without excuse.

Every single human being who has ever lived is without excuse. They *can* know there is a God. I know that's a strong statement, but it's what the Bible says. Paul is clear here that what can be known about God is evident in His creation if we only have eyes to see. R. C. Sproul says,

> The knowledge God gives of Himself is not obscure. It is not buried with hidden clues that only an intellectual, elite group of people are able to discover. . . . The truth God gives of Himself is manifest. It is clear—so plain that everybody gets it.[1]

The first step in this eye-opening experience is for our boys to acknowledge there is a God, and there's no better way a mom can make that easy for them than to show them the beauty of God's creation. If I asked my boys right now what the rainbow is a symbol of, I hope they would say it's a promise that God will never flood the earth again. The reason I hope they'll say that is because for their entire lives, I've pointed out rainbows and *told* them what they symbolize. I've pointed out glorious sunsets and said, "Look, son! The God of the Universe, Who created that sunset, loves YOU. Isn't that amazing?" I've bent down in the sand and pointed to the ocean and said, "Listen, boys. Can you hear the sound of the water? Can you feel its power? This is what the Bible tells us the voice of God sounds like!" When we're driving in the car together—a rarity these days that I always try to make use of—I do my best to point out the handiwork of God. I've done this for their entire lives, and while I admittedly don't always get the profound response from teenage boys that I hope for, my intent is to paint a picture so vibrant and vivid in their minds that knowing God exists will never be a question they have to answer. They'll just believe.

This way of casting the vision can work beyond God's amazing creation as well. Just the other day my older son got a piece of good news. Something he'd been hoping for fell into place because someone he knew and had a relationship with was able to make a connection for him. When he called to tell me about it, he said, "Man, I just got lucky!" I quickly replied, "I don't believe in luck, buddy. I believe in the hand of God moving you exactly where He wants you to be."

Creating a worldview for our boys takes time and intention. I've been doing this for years with the goal of helping them to see things God's way instead of their own. I'm constantly pointing them back to the truth of God's Word. Sometimes they hear and receive it, and other times I have to trust that God is planting a seed in their hearts that He intends to grow later. As my friend Teri Lynne Underwood says, "Parenting is the long game." We make millions of tiny investments in the lives and hearts of our children while they're in our home and trust God to make the best of it in spite of our shortcomings. Our goal is to make it as easy as possible for them to see and know there is a God. It's God's job to do the rest.

It's worth noting that parenting this way isn't solely done to help our children see and know God. Living from a God-centered perspective will give them better, more meaningful lives. Not better in the sense that they'll have more things or be successful as the world defines success, but their lives will consist of a deeper quality of character and understanding of the world around them. But even with all these intentional actions and conversations, there remains the knowledge that if God doesn't show up, nothing happens.

Ephesians 1:17–19 says

I pray that the God of our Lord Jesus Christ, the glorious Father, would give you the Spirit of wisdom and revelation in the knowledge of him. *I pray that the eyes of your heart may be enlightened so that you may know what is the hope of his calling*, what is the wealth of his glorious inheritance in the saints, and what is the immeasurable greatness of his power toward us who believe, according to the mighty working of his strength. (emphasis mine)

I clearly remember the day God taught me that He is the one who changes hearts of stone to hearts of flesh. If you read *Praying for Boys*, my first book, you remember the story well. I shared a piece of it in chapter 3 of this book, but it was such a before-and-after moment for me that I want to share it again here.

I don't know why I was studying in Ezekiel during that time in my life. The boys were very young, and I was just beginning to catch a glimpse of what it was going to require of me to create the life I wanted for my family. For whatever reason, though, Ezekiel 36:26 grabbed my heart in one of those pivotal, life-changing moments. It says, "I will give you a new heart and put a new spirit within you; I will remove your heart of stone and give you a heart of flesh." In an instant, my eyes were opened to the fact that God is the one who changes hearts of stone to hearts of flesh. I could partner with Him in making it as easy as possible for them to know the truth of their need for a Savior, but I could never make them choose Jesus. That is God's job alone. So from that time forward, I prayed for God to open the eyes of their understanding and turn their hearts of stone to hearts of flesh.

Having eyes to see means more than just knowing a God exists. It means surrendering their lives to that God through relationship with His Son, Jesus. This is the goal of any Christian parent, but it isn't something we can achieve on our own. At times, I've felt very grateful for that . . . even relieved that the weight of their salvation doesn't fall solely on my shoulders. I'd mess it up for sure. But at other times, I've wished I could snap my fingers and just force them to see what I see, know what I know, and act accordingly. Unfortunately, that's not the way it works, and until our children know Jesus, we can't expect them to act like Christians.

Mom, if you're reading this right now with a child who has not yet come to faith in Jesus, or if your child has walked away from the faith and is currently breaking your heart with his choices, know this: Prayer is the best gift you can give him. God's Word is living and active (Hebrews 4:12 ESV). It has the power to change a human heart from the inside out, and it will do exactly what God purposes for it to do (Isaiah 55:11). Put all your faith in that truth. There is nothing more powerful than praying God's Word over our children. When we do, we're planting seeds. God may bring other people into their lives to water those seeds. The fruition of our prayers may or may not happen when we can see it, but rest assured that God hears your fervent prayers and is acting with compassion toward you and your children (Psalm 40:11), and it's His kindness that will lead them to repentance (Romans 2:4).

A Changed Perspective

One of the hardest lessons for boys is learning to think about someone other than themselves. Nashville-based counselor David Thomas once told me that teenage boys are the most self-centered people he knows, and I agree. The reason for this, David said, is because of the natural development of parts of their brain and emotions. It isn't always that they're trying to be selfish and self-centered. It's that for the first time they are aware of all the working pieces of their lives. They're aware of their appearance and what people think about them and can easily become consumed with it. We talked about the importance of teaching boys to be humble in chapters 3 and 6, so I won't repeat myself, but it's worth another quick glance in this spot because the truth is that teenage boys won't naturally put others above themselves. Sure, some people have naturally giving, sacrificial personalities, but most of us, girls included, come out of the womb incredibly selfish. Humility, which Philippians 2:3 defines as seeing others as more important than ourselves, requires a submitted relationship with Christ—a clear understanding of how He gave Himself up for us that inspires us to do the same for others. It comes after a decision to follow Christ, so I include here a slightly deeper look at it through the Old Testament story of the prophet Elisha.

Elisha was the man who took up the mantle of prophet to Israel after the prophet Elijah. Sometimes it's hard to remember who's who so think of it this way: Elijah revived a widow's son who had died (1 Kings 17:17–24), challenged the priests of Baal to a contest on Mount Carmel (1 Kings 18:20–40), and went up to heaven in a chariot of fire (2 Kings 2:11). According to Scripture, Elisha received a double portion of Elijah's power (2 Kings 2:9) and is known for the miracle of multiplying a widow's jar of oil (2 Kings 4:1–7). He performed miracles that were like Elijah's, but far greater in number.

In 2 Kings 6 we find Elisha facing war between God's people and the king of Syria. In a season when most of God's people weren't living faithful lives, He still actively cared for them by giving Elisha the battle plan of the enemy. (There's a word there for your wayward boys, Mom. Even when they're unfaithful, God never is.) This allowed the armies of Israel to be prepared and have the upper hand, insight any of us might wish to have when facing life's battles. When a great army of Syria moved against Israel, encamping around them in the night and surrounding the city where Elisha was, Elisha's servant became very afraid. But there was something he could not see that Elisha could.

> Elisha said, "Don't be afraid, for those who are with us outnumber those who are with them." Then Elisha prayed, "Lord, please open his eyes and let him see." So the Lord opened the servant's eyes, and he saw that the mountain was covered with horses and chariots of fire all around Elisha.
>
> 2 Kings 6:16–17

What the servant saw was a great enemy army surrounding him. What he couldn't see, that is until Elisha prayed, was the army of God there as well ready to do battle on his behalf.

I don't know about you, but that fills me with mad faith. In fact, I want to jump up and down and scream "GO GOD!"

when I read this story because it's absolute proof that God is fighting for us, and for our children, even if we can't see it. *Lord! Open our eyes to see you all around us!*

But as much as I want to get lost in the moment, like God is the winning team during a high school football game, there's more to this idea of having our eyes opened than just chariots of fire. There is much God is doing in this world that happens without our knowledge or permission, so we must ask God to help us see the world His way. This is another reason to point out the Creator to our kids and pray Scripture over them. If they don't have God's perspective, they won't have the full life Jesus died to give them. Elisha knew that if he could help his servant see the truth, it would change his perspective, and it certainly did. The knowledge that God is powerfully working for us changes the way we feel, the things we do, and the way we think. This is true for us, and it is true for our sons. God gave Elisha and his servant a powerful, dynamic visual to demonstrate that there's more going on in the spiritual realm than meets the eye, but did you catch Elisha's order of priority?

If I were Elisha, I might've been tempted to panic first when I saw the enemy surrounding me. In fact, I know I would have, because that's my tendency. I panic first, then start speaking God's truth to myself until my heart slows down. For special occasions, when even this doesn't ease my stress, I worship. Somehow, singing to God accomplishes something words alone can't, and it usually helps me re-center myself on God so that I can see things His way again. But that's not what happened to Elisha in this moment.

Instead of panicking or worrying at all about himself, Elisha calmly showed concern for his servant's fear. He knew that his servant needed to learn to trust the Lord in difficult situations, especially when he couldn't see the full picture. At the time of this miraculous event, Elisha had a depth in his relationship with God that his servant didn't. This gave him the ability not only to control his own response, but to see his servant's need and meet it. This is the kind of depth we must pray God develops in our sons.

One of my boys was heavily involved in Young Life throughout his high school career. If you're not familiar with Young Life, its mission is to introduce adolescents to Jesus Christ and help them grow in their faith. One summer, just a few days before he left for Young Life camp, his school representative told him they had a few spots still open and asked if he knew anyone who might be able to come at the last minute. In a matter of about two hours, he had invited several of his friends to pack up and get on the road, and one of those friends gave his life to Christ at camp that week. I don't know if my son would have thought to invite those friends on his own, but with his Young Life representative's encouragement he got to be a part of a life-changing work of God. He can see the change in this young man's life, and it serves as a constant reminder about the influence he has when he simply stops to think about others.

God Will Do the Work

Philippians 3:15–16 says, "Therefore, let all of us who are mature think this way. And if you think differently about anything, God will reveal this also to you. In any case, we should live up to whatever truth we have attained."

It struck me that this is exactly what parents experience as they watch their children mature in their relationship with Christ. We watch them embrace a knowledge of their Creator, pray for them to see their great need for a Savior, and then watch them grow in it until they are men who serve those around them with the love of Christ. That process might take years. In fact, we might not live to see the end of the process. We may wish they had the same experiential knowledge of Christ, and a deeper, mature relationship with Christ like ours right now, but they don't. They can't. Most of what we can do as parents is pray that God will reveal truth to our kids if their thinking is immature in some way. And by immature, I don't really mean wrong. It isn't wrong to be a teenage Christian with a limited perspective on life. It isn't wrong to have only walked with the Lord for a few years and have a long way to go in maturing in Him. I'm in my forties and I still have a long way to go. The right thing is for all of us to live up to whatever truth we have attained today, and pray for God to give us, and our kids, more truth tomorrow.

"LORD, OPEN HIS EYES" PRAYERS

Romans 1:18–20—"For God's wrath is revealed from heaven against all godlessness and unrighteousness of people who by their unrighteousness suppress the truth, since what can be known about God is evident among them, because God has shown it to them. For his invisible attributes, that is, his eternal power and divine nature, have been clearly seen since the creation of the world, being understood through what he has made. As a result, people are without excuse."

> **PRAYER:** Father, give _____ eyes to see that which you have already made plain. May he embrace you as the Creator of the world and see your hand behind everything that has been made. In Jesus' name, Amen.

Ephesians 1:17—"I pray that the God of our Lord Jesus Christ, the glorious Father, would give you the Spirit of wisdom and revelation in the knowledge of him."

PRAYER: Lord, give _____ the Spirit of wisdom and revelation, so that he may know you as well as possible. In Jesus'
name, Amen.

Ezekiel 36:26—"I will give you a new heart and put a new
spirit within you; I will remove your heart of stone and give
you a heart of flesh."

PRAYER: Lord, soften_____'s heart, and place a new
spirit within him. Give him a heart of flesh so that he can follow
you. In Jesus' name, Amen.

Hebrews 4:12—"For the word of God is living and effective
and sharper than any double-edged sword, penetrating as far
as the separation of soul and spirit, joints and marrow. It is
able to judge the thoughts and intentions of the heart."

PRAYER: Lord, make your Word alive for my son. Draw him to
it. Fascinate him with its truth. Cause it to judge the thoughts
and intentions of his heart so that he can confess sin and follow
you with a pure heart. In Jesus' name, Amen.

Isaiah 55:11—"My word that comes from my mouth will not
return to me empty, but it will accomplish what I please and
will prosper in what I send it to do."

PRAYER: Lord, I believe your Word will do exactly what you
want it to do. Make it achieve your purposes in and through
_____. In Jesus' name, Amen.

Philippians 2:3—"Do nothing out of selfish ambition or conceit, but in humility consider others as more important than
yourselves."

PRAYER: Father, help _____ to see other people the way you see them, and give him the desire to serve them so they can see you in him. Help him lay down selfish ambition and vain conceit, and embrace humility instead. In Jesus' name, Amen.

Philippians 3:15–16—"Therefore, let all of us who are mature think this way. And if you think differently about anything, God will reveal this also to you. In any case, we should live up to whatever truth we have attained."

PRAYER: Lord, mature _____ in his faith in you. Where he doesn't see things the way you do, open his eyes and make it clear. In Jesus' name, Amen.

Psalm 119:18—"Open my eyes so that I may contemplate wondrous things from your instruction."

PRAYER: Father, open my son's eyes to see how wonderful your ways are. Give him the understanding that patterning his life after you is true freedom. In Jesus' name, Amen.

Isaiah 50:4—"The LORD GOD has given me the tongue of those who are instructed to know how to sustain the weary with a word. He awakens me each morning; he awakens my ear to listen like those being instructed."

PRAYER: Father, give _____ the ability to use his words to bring life to others. Waken his ears to listen to your instruction so that he can use his mouth to bring blessing to those around him. In Jesus' name, Amen.

Acts 26:17–18—"I am sending you to them to open their eyes so that they may turn from darkness to light and from the power of Satan to God, that they may receive forgiveness of sins and a share among those who are sanctified by faith in me."

PRAYER: Father, open _____'s eyes. Turn his heart from darkness to light. Lead him to put his faith and trust in Jesus as his Savior so that he may receive forgiveness of sins and a place among the sanctified. In Jesus' name, Amen.

PRAYERS AND NOTES

8

LORD, GIVE HIM A HEART AFTER YOU

Hundreds, if not thousands, of authors and pastors before me have written about some aspect of King David's life. I'm not sure I'll have anything to say about him here that you haven't heard at least touched on before. But I hope to help you see one part of his character that has a direct correlation to our prayers for our sons a bit clearer than you have before. There's a reason he's one of the most beloved characters of Scripture, and that makes him a perfect fit for this chapter. David messed up time and time again. He made choices and mistakes that make him seem relatable, easy to love, and in a word, *human*. We can relate to his passion and his falls from glory. But what distinguishes David from other biblical characters is that somehow, he always came back to his fervent, devoted love for God. He had a heart *after* God (1 Samuel 13:14), and this is a character trait we want our boys to possess.

I've read much online debate about what exactly it means to have a heart after God. Some have speculated that David's heart was like God's, but that's hard to justify because as much as David loved the Lord, he was also a pretty radical sinner. I'm not sure any of us have a heart *like* God's. We may be created in His image, but His heart is pure, while ours is "deceitful above all things" (Jeremiah 17:9 ESV), making our heart and God's heart opposites without Christ. Adultery, murder, and deceit were just a few of the actions that darkened David's heart.

Another viewpoint is that the words "after his own heart" in 1 Samuel 13 simply meant God would be the one to choose the king this time. He let the people choose the first king, Saul, and that didn't go well. David might simply have been God's choice as opposed to the peoples' choice, but I believe a better way to understand the kind of heart David had is that God was looking for a man who would "carry out all my will" (Acts 13:22). David's heart longed to pursue and *run after* God, and that's exactly what He needed in a king.

One of my new favorite shows is *Sullivan's Crossing*. *Gilmore Girls* fans will immediately recognize the title character, Sully, as Luke Danes, Lorelai Gilmore's main love interest. There's a flashback scene that happens often in the first season (which is all I've seen so far) that reminds me of what it is to be *after* God's heart. It occurs as Maggie, the main female character, is being dragged to her mother's car kicking and screaming, away from her father, Sully. It's clear that there's been a split between the two parents, and as the show develops, we learn it's because Maggie's mom felt the "simple" life Sully could offer them at Sullivan's Crossing wasn't good enough for her and wouldn't be a good enough place to raise their daughter. She drags her to the car and shoves her into the back seat, peeling out of the driveway while young Maggie is screaming for her daddy.

Sully tries to catch them, but to no avail (I won't spoil what happens next), and I imagine this, while a sad version of what I'm hoping to illustrate, is what it feels like to run after something of the utmost importance. Sully's daughter was the most important thing in the world to him, and he wanted more than anything to run after her, to get her back, and to be in right, restored relationship with her. He, like David, might've tripped, stumbled, or hit some bumps along the way, but the deepest longing of his heart was to go *after* the object of his love. So it was with David's love for God, and that's what God was looking for in a king. I think it's also what He's looking for in each of us.

In First Samuel 13, we see the prophet Samuel informing the current king, Saul, that God has rejected him. Even though it will be many more years before David takes the throne as the second king of Israel, God chooses him because of the kind of heart he has. Not because he never messed up—God knew he had. Not because he did not sin—God knew he would. But because despite David's humanness, the inclination of his heart was to follow God with abandon. Proverbs 3:5–6 instructs us to "Trust in the Lord with all your heart, and do not rely on your own understanding; in all your ways know him, and he will make your paths straight." It was only in the moments when David chose to rely on his own strength that his life went awry. Even when his sin found him out, the immediate response of his heart was to fall on his face and repent. Listen to his words in Psalm 51, right after the Lord used the prophet Nathan to expose his grievous sin:

> Be gracious to me, God, according to your faithful love; according to your abundant compassion, blot out my rebellion. Completely wash away my guilt and cleanse me from my sin. For I am conscious of my rebellion, and my sin is always before me. Against you—you alone—I have sinned and done this evil in your sight.

vv. 1–4

David's response to the sins of adultery, murder, and deceit didn't eliminate the consequences of those sins, but it did restore right relationship between him and God. David's heart always seemed inclined toward reconciliation. This is the reason God could use him. This is the reason God chose him.

Can the same thing be said of us? Despite his royal mess-ups, I believe David loved the Lord his God with all his heart and with all his soul and with all his strength and with all his mind (Luke 10:27) . . . at least as well as anyone could. Our sons, like David, will mess up. I hope they won't commit murder or adultery, but they will sin, repeatedly. Having a heart after God's means that when they do, they'll know and love God well enough to sincerely repent, running away from sin and toward God.

But what does God's heart look like? How can we help set the bar for excellence in our boys' lives so that they know what they're chasing after? That's what we're going to explore in this chapter.

The Heart of God

One summer day my son and two of his friends decided to take the four-wheelers for a ride on my mom and dad's property. They live on about five acres that is mostly wooded and mostly uphill, but there are rough roads that take you all the way to the top next to the water tower for our town. The view from up there is spectacular, giving you a unique perspective on almost the entire town. Those rough roads are perfect for four-wheelers and have outlets in several places in the neighborhood, so riding makes for a fun afternoon.

My husband and I don't own any four-wheelers, so when my boys want the adventure they use the ones that belong to my mom and dad. They have one old red one that they bought over twenty years ago and a newer green one that is bigger, more powerful, and automatic. That day, after my son and his two friends finished working for our town's rec department building fences at the baseball fields, they decided to take a ride. With my parents' permission, my son hopped on a machine that belonged to his grandparents, one of his friends hopped on the other, and a third friend had his dad bring their four-wheeler so he could ride along.

In their excitement and thrill at the speed under their control, they got separated, and the friend who had the least experience riding four-wheelers had an accident. Thankfully, it wasn't a bad accident, but he did lose control of the four-wheeler and turn it over on his ankle. He limped for a day or two and then was fine. My son also hit something while driving the four-wheeler too fast and damaged the body of the machine. It was stressful for us because our son and his friends were involved, but it was even more stressful for us because we felt like our son disrespected the expensive equipment his grandparents made available to him and his friends. We would still have been upset if the four-wheelers had belonged to us. We were more upset with him because they didn't.

My son loves his grandfather. Both of my parents have played a significant role in my children's lives and have been more than generous to them over the years. It was because of that deep love my son has for my dad that he was so disgusted with himself. He knew he had disappointed his grandfather, and that might've been harder to bear than the fact that he would have to pay for the damages. After making sure everyone was safe, my husband gave my son an earful in my parents' driveway in front of his friends. Maybe that's why my dad responded the way he did. Or maybe it's just because this is an area where my dad has consistently shown his family the heart of God.

A few hours after the incident, once both of the other boys had gotten safely home and the four-wheelers were cleaned up and put away, I took the lead instigator back up to my parents' house so he could formally apologize and accept his punishment. I intended to make him repay every dollar required to fix the machines he was responsible for that day. He had a job, and as far as I was concerned, every dollar was going straight to my parents for the rest of the summer. But as my son sat in the family room of the house I grew up in, truly repentant, choking back tears, and telling his grandparents how sorry he was, I saw my dad's composure start to soften. It was a look I recognized clearly, and I knew I was getting ready to witness the compassion and generosity that had been extended to me as a child many times.

My dad is a master at taking life circumstances and using them to teach a lesson, and as I looked on from the couch, he offered that gift to his grandson. He could have raged. He had every right to be upset. No one would have been surprised had he opened his computer and made a spreadsheet to help track expenses and keep up with what our son owed. But that's not what he did. He offered grace and the opportunity for my son to leave the situation in right relationship with his grandparents. Instead of having to pay back any money, he worked off the damages weeding in my mom's garden and playing chess and pool with my dad for a few hours each week. He maintained his dignity (and his money) while my dad found a way to build the relationship and make him feel safe. I think that's a perfect representation of the heart of God to His children.

God's heart—the character traits that describe the way He acts throughout history—is summed up in Psalm 86:15: "But you, Lord, are a compassionate and gracious God, slow to anger and abounding in faithful love and truth."

Slow to Anger

When we got back to our house that night, I pulled my husband aside and said, "I'm glad it happened. Not that anyone was hurt, or that the machines are damaged, but that he got to see this side of my dad. I never once felt unsafe going to my dad when I messed up as a kid. I didn't have to hide. I knew he was safe, and that he would have my back no matter what, and I'm so grateful our son got to experience that for himself."

To be honest, my husband and I had probably showed our son enough anger for everyone involved that day, and we weren't slow about it. If there's anything we know about the God we read about in the Old Testament, it's that He can get angry. But God's anger, as opposed to ours, is justified and righteous, and it comes in response to sin. According to the Reverend Billy Graham, "When the Bible tells us that God 'is slow to anger' (Nahum 1:3), it simply means that He is patient beyond man's capability. It takes a great deal to stir God's anger—but when it happens, it is holy anger because God is pure and righteous."[1]

I've read some accounts of God's anger in the Bible—like the story of Sodom and Gomorrah or Jonah and the Ninevites—and wondered why His response had to be the way it was. There were times when His anger against sin wiped out entire cities, women and children included. His reaction seems quick to me, but the truth is that God possesses immense patience. Even with Sodom his patience is on display as he tells Abraham he is willing to spare it from destruction if he can only find ten righteous people living there (Genesis 18).

Jonah, called to preach repentance to the dreaded Ninevites, received a second chance from God after running away in disobedience. This is the very definition of the word *longsuffering*. God was willing to wait until Jonah's heart was ready, no matter what it took, and even when it seemed like all hope was lost, He provided a way. If God seems in Scripture to move fast it's because He had been patient for long enough, or because the sin was just too grievous, and the time for patience had passed. Second Peter 3:9 tells us that "the Lord does not delay his promise, as some understand delay, but is patient with you, not wanting any to perish but all to come to repentance." We can trust the timing of His anger, knowing that He sees the big picture of eternity past and eternity future.

There's something here for our boys.

The world is going to press them. By that, I just mean that there will be plenty of opportunities for them to be quick to anger instead of slow. But the Scriptures advise against this. James 1:19–20 says, "My dear brothers and sisters, understand this: Everyone should be quick to listen, slow to speak, and slow to anger, for human anger does not accomplish God's righteousness." This is because having a quick trigger toward anger doesn't represent the heart of God.

Faithful

To be faithful means to be true to one's word or promises, steady, trustworthy, believable, and reliable. Anyone can make it their goal to be faithful, but unlike God, they will, at times, fail to keep their promises. God is the only one who will always keep His promises, always be faithful, and always be and do what He says He will. We can have faith in the faithfulness of God, but it isn't always easy.

My friend Erin Warren, in her book *Everyday Prayers for Faith*, tells of a season when her faith in God's faithfulness began to waver. Her husband, Kris, was very sick, and would likely never be healed this side of heaven. She listened as other believers reminded her that God would be faithful and found herself pondering how quick we are to applaud God's faithfulness when

He gives us what we want, and how quick we are to question it when He doesn't. When we get a healthy diagnosis, we praise God for being faithful. When we ask for relief, and it comes, we sing of His faithfulness. But what about when He doesn't immediately, or ever, give us what we want? Is He still faithful then? Can we still sing of standing on God's promises when they don't seem to be that solid? Do we even understand what God's promises are? Erin said, "God is faithful, and God doesn't change. I knew that. So I started wondering if I had misunderstood the meaning of His faithfulness."[2]

One of the mistakes we make as humans is putting our faith in things that never made and can't keep promises to us.[3] But we can build our lives on the promises of God. They will never fail us. According to one source,[4] there are over seven thousand promises of God in the Bible, and we can trust Him to be faithful to each one. In fact, as we look back at Scripture and see how God was faithful to His promises, it fills us with faith that He will do the same for us. He is the same God yesterday, today, and forever (Hebrews 13:8), and when God proves Himself faithful to us by keeping His promises, it makes it easier to believe He will do it again.

In the case of my son and my father, there was an unspoken promise. Not a promise with the bond or power of one made by God, but one where my dad cared for my son's heart more than he did his own possessions. In this way, Dad showed that he was a man who could be trusted. He was true to his word, true to who he said he would be, and true to how he promised to react should difficult things come. This is a direct reflection of the heart of God in him, and it's an example of how this works. As our sons see what God's heart looks like in those around them, it becomes attractive to them. More than that, it powerfully moves them in those times of their lives when they are most open and in need of it.

Loving

The world defines love as an intense feeling of deep affection. If that's accurate, I love my dogs, my cat, my family, my heated blanket, and my milk frother. I do have intense feelings of deep affection for all of these things, but it's plain to see that I don't love them all the same. As a culture, we throw the word *love* around too easily. It might be better to say that I love my family (and animals), and really enjoy my heated blanket and milk frother, but there is another definition of love that's even more important for us and our boys. I shared it in *Praying for Boys*:

> The Bible says, "God *is* love" (1 John 4:8). For you mathematicians, using the word *is* is the same as using the word *equals*. In other words, God and love are one and the same. God = Love. There is no real love apart from God, and God is behind all genuine acts of love. . . . Men tend to equate love with the physical, women the emotional. And certainly the fullness of God's nature is found in both aspects of love. But without God, love is often reduced to superficial, self-serving, pleasure-seeking feelings.[5]

Kind of puts my frothy coffee under a warm heated blanket in a different light.

As I'm writing this chapter, there are only thirteen days until Christmas. One of the truths I've been trying to help my family embrace this year is a simple expansion of what we normally focus on at Christmas. We celebrate that Jesus came every year. God sent a baby, born of a virgin, to save the world. But it's more than that. Jesus didn't just come. He came for *me*. He came for *you*. It's so very personal. When we sing "Away in a Manger" without internalizing this important truth, it's easier to keep the love of God at bay, as if it's for someone else instead of for us. We give an intellectual nod and say, "Yes, Jesus came at Christmas. I believe," and then move on with the rest of our lives.

But celebrating the birth of Christ is much more than that. It's about a love so deep, so wide, so far-reaching that it changed the course of history, and it should change the course of our lives.

The day of the wreck, my son was loving himself more than anything and anyone else. And honestly, I didn't have to tell him that. He knew it, and I believe the fact that he did is what enabled my dad to offer him such grace. This is the example of love we're given between the Father and His Son, and it's how we should explain and define love for our sons.

Merciful

Initially, I wanted to punish my son for the wreck, or rather, I wanted my dad to punish him for what I saw as a careless attitude toward an expensive piece of equipment that didn't belong to him. But my dad extended mercy to his grandson instead. Mercy, as defined in a biblical sense, basically means not getting the punishment we deserve. All of us deserve to be punished for our sins. The ultimate punishment is spending all of eternity in hell apart from God, but even the "little" things are enough to separate us. God is holy, and He can't be in the presence of sin. That's why we needed a Savior.

Because He is rich in mercy (Ephesians 2:4–5), God makes a habit of not giving us what we deserve, and that's exactly what my dad did for my son. He deserved to have to pay for the full damages to both four-wheelers, but instead, my dad let him work it off in the backyard over the rest of the summer. He trusted and hoped that mercy would have more of an impact on his heart than punishment, and it did.

Slow anger, faithfulness, sacrificial love, mercy . . . these are the character traits that display who God is, and they're what we can hope to teach and model for our boys so they can have a heart *after* His.

"LORD, GIVE HIM A HEART AFTER YOU" PRAYERS

First Samuel 13:14—"But now your reign will not endure. The LORD has found a man after his own heart, and the LORD has appointed him as ruler over his people, because you have not done what the LORD commanded."

PRAYER: Father, make _____ a man after your own heart. Teach him to go out of his way to do all of your will so that you can use him for your glory. In Jesus' name, Amen.

Psalm 86:15—"But you, Lord, are a compassionate and gracious God, slow to anger and abounding in faithful love and truth."

PRAYER: Lord, thank you for who you are. Be gracious and compassionate to _____ as he learns to walk with you. Abound in love and faithfulness to him. In Jesus' name, Amen.

Psalm 103:11–12—"For as high as the heavens are above the earth, so great is his faithful love toward those who fear him. As far as the east is from the west, so far has he removed our transgressions from us."

PRAYER: Father, make _____ to fear you. Help him to see and know how deeply he is loved by you, and to hold in high esteem what it cost you to forgive him for his sins. In Jesus' name, Amen.

Ephesians 2:14—"For he is our peace, who made both groups one and tore down the dividing wall of hostility."

PRAYER: Lord, be _____'s peace. In a world that wants to steal and corrupt what belongs to him, remind him of who you are and to seek you for the peace he needs. In Jesus' name, Amen.

Proverbs 3:6—"In all your ways know him, and he will make your paths straight."

PRAYER: Lord, turn _____'s eyes to you. Teach him the value of submitting his ways to your plan, and keep him on the straight path. In Jesus' name, Amen.

Lamentations 3:22–23—"Because of the LORD's faithful love we do not perish, for his mercies never end. They are new every morning; great is your faithfulness!"

PRAYER: Lord, thank you for new morning mercies. When _____ sins against you, remind him of your great love for him. Your compassions never fail. Be faithful to him. In Jesus' name, Amen.

John 16:33—"I have told you these things so that in me you may have peace. You will have suffering in this world. Be courageous! I have conquered the world."

PRAYER: Lord, help _____ to remember that Christians are not exempt from struggle. In fact, you promised us we would have troubles. Teach him to find his peace in you, the one who overcomes. In Jesus' name, Amen.

Psalm 25:5—"Guide me in your truth and teach me, for you are the God of my salvation; I wait for you all day long."

PRAYER: Lord, guide _____ in your truth and teach him, for you are God his Savior. May his hope be in you all day long. In Jesus' name, Amen.

Philippians 2:13—"For it is God who is working in you both to will and to work according to his good purpose."

PRAYER: Lord, work in _____. Help him to see your hand in his life acting in order to fulfill your good purpose for him. In Jesus' name, Amen.

John 3:16—"For God loved the world in this way: He gave his one and only Son, so that everyone who believes in him will not perish but have eternal life."

PRAYER: Lord, open _____'s eyes to see Jesus as the only way to the Father. May he know in his heart that God loved him enough to send a Savior just for him. Work in him to believe so that he might not perish but have eternal life. In Jesus' name, Amen.

PRAYERS AND NOTES

9

LORD, MAKE THE
HIDDEN THINGS KNOWN

For my dad's seventieth birthday, my brother and I planned a roasting. I cleaned my house for a week before our entire family descended upon us, fixed all his favorite foods, and then sat back and watched as his brothers, nephews, niece, and son told stories on him and each other that made my belly hurt from laughter.

I'm the baby of the family, so by the time I was old enough to get into trouble I knew better. I had watched the adventures of my older sibling and cousins and thought I knew all the stories that would be told that day . . . but I was wrong. For hours, my dad's older and younger brothers told stories on each other that I had never heard. And when the cousins started chiming in, I heard stories on them I had never heard before, and by the looks on their faces, their parents hadn't either. Most revolved around pushing favorite cars to the limits, and thankfully, the statute of limitations had run out on their ability to be punished for some of that outrageousness. It's easier to laugh after twenty years have passed than it is in the moment. We learned all kinds of things about each other that day, hilarious family stories my husband and I have shared with our boys now that both of my uncles have passed. But the main takeaway was that your deeds will always find you out (Numbers 32:23), even if it's many years down the road.

On Letting Go

One of the hardest parts of being a parent of a young adult is balancing their freedom with continued parenting responsibility. My husband and I felt that keenly when our older son left our home for the first time right after graduating from high school, and then again when he left for college. He was only a little over an hour away from us. We could get to him easily if we were needed, or even just because we wanted to see him. But the big, gaping hole we had to learn to deal with—which just might have been the hardest part of releasing a young adult into the wild—was that we had no control over how he spent his time.

While he was in high school, we didn't always know what he was doing, but we certainly knew where he was. And we also knew that if he did anything bad enough, we would hear about it almost immediately from school officials. Thankfully, that didn't happen often. While in school, even when their lives began to separate from ours more and more, our sons still come home every night and sleep under our roof. There's a comfort in knowing they're safely in their rooms, even if we didn't see them much that day. There's a sense of safety that comes when we have the right to tell them what time to be home and enforce consequences when they fall short.

Our son's senior year of high school was a tremendous learning opportunity for us, as it is with most parents of first-borns, and it brought with it a sense of ripping away. Not only did his schedule keep him from us—sports practices, senior activities, and time with friends and girlfriends—but his whole being began to turn in a different direction, sometimes painfully. Not a turning away from us because of an offense, but a turning toward the man he was becoming apart from his family of origin. It's called differentiation, and it's the process of learning who you are as a person separate from who you are or have been with your family. It's supposed to happen, but living it can be hard. We didn't always do everything right (and he'd freely tell you that!), and we sometimes acted out of fear instead of trust and faith. But God taught us much through the process.

This season was the beginning of learning to trust God for our older son. Many, many times I asked myself if we had done enough, taught him enough, tried hard enough. I've come to understand that the answer for all families to this question is likely no. Even those who do their very best—better than we have—will leave some things out. There will always be more we could've done, and learning to trust God involves releasing those things to Him. It also includes releasing control of their schedules. The reality was that while he was at college, we had to trust that he could and would make good decisions, because we had zero control over things like parties, curfews, who he chose to befriend, and what time he went to bed.

The feelings of helplessness this caused in both my husband and me led me to pray frequently that God would show us things we couldn't see with our own eyes. I prayed for our son to be held accountable by God Himself in the times when it was impossible for me to hold him accountable. I prayed for God to reveal areas of sin that might be hard to see on his short visits home during the semester, and I prayed that He would do it in a way and at a time that provided the most benefit to our son. Our God is in heaven and does as He pleases (Psalm 115:3), when He pleases, but we can ask Him to reveal to us what we need to know. These may not be easy prayers, and the answers to them aren't always easy either. If we're going to pray this way, we have to be prepared for God to show us what we want to know, even if it isn't pretty.

Accountability

I decided recently to try something I've never been able to accomplish before: reading through the Bible in ninety days. I tried once when my children were very young and I was still working part-time outside of the home, and it was a disaster. I failed in every way, giving up within just a couple of days. I've read the Bible many times, but never that quickly straight through. I was intrigued by the idea of seeing connections a slower reading might hide and looking at the Bible as the cohesive story of God unfolding. I wanted a big picture to go along with my years of smaller, more intimate study of limited passages. So when my friend Mary DeMuth announced that she was leading a 90-day read-through of the Bible starting January 1, I knew I wanted to try. As I write this, I have just finished the book of Genesis (50 chapters) in four days, and I've learned things I did not know before, or at the very least had forgotten. But the story that sticks out to me the most, and that beautifully illustrates the idea of God making hidden things known, is that of Joseph.

Joseph's father, Jacob, had two wives (Rachel and Leah), and two concubines, who all gave him sons. But Joseph, one of the two youngest of his twelve sons, was Jacob's favorite (most likely because Joseph's mother, Rachel, was his true love). Jacob was the son of Isaac and Rebekah, and Isaac the promised son of Abraham and Sarah. When Scripture refers to the "God of Abraham, Isaac, and Jacob," this is the family it's describing—God's chosen among the nations, those who received special favor from God, and who would eventually become God's chosen people, the nation of Israel.

Joseph made it possible for the plans of God to be accomplished for his people, so he's very important, but because of his father's special affection for him, Joseph was hated by his brothers. Genesis 37 tells the story of their hatred of him in great detail, culminating in a scheme to sell him into slavery and make Jacob, their father (later renamed Israel) believe he had been killed viciously by an animal. It's a wild story that would make a casual reader scratch her head and wonder how in the world God could let something like that happen to an "innocent" teenage boy. (I put *innocent* in quotes because I've never known a completely innocent teenage boy, and Joseph could've made life a bit easier on himself along the way.) But as always, God turns what's meant for evil into something good, and this story is no exception.

One of the most difficult transitions into manhood involves being accountable for our own actions. My sons have had a favorite excuse over the years that my husband and I have shot down time and time again. When something happens that's their fault, they'll say, "I didn't mean to." What they mean by that is that they didn't do anything to hurt anyone or get in trouble on purpose, and I believe that. The problem with this way of thinking is that it doesn't remove fault from them. When I was in my early thirties, I rear-ended a truck stopped at a stoplight. I didn't mean to hit the truck. In fact, I wished very much that I hadn't, but it was still my fault, and the accountability for what followed rested squarely on me. Joseph's brothers were accountable for him, both as one of the youngest of the brothers in need of protection and guidance, and because the day they sold him into slavery Jacob had sent Joseph to them on his behalf. The difference between them and me is that they meant to hurt him, and frankly, thought they had gotten away with it.

But they hadn't, because God knew.

It's fascinating how God uses our sinful choices to further His plans, but He does. Truly, He works all things together for the good of those who love Him and are called according to His purposes (Romans 8:28). Not *some* things. Not *some* things, *some*times. *All* things at *all* times bow to the authority and will of God the Father. Joseph's brothers temporarily forgot that actions have consequences, even if it takes years for them to come to fruition. I look back on my own life and can clearly remember times when I thought I was getting away with something wrong, and even though my sins weren't always found out publicly (because God is gracious and kind), there was never, not one single time that I sinned against God or someone else that HE didn't see it happen. Now, in my mid-forties, that somehow feels worse. Why? Because I know that my choices to sin weren't only or even mainly against another person. They were mainly against God Himself. And as a more mature Christian now, someone who realizes the depth of my sin and the depth of God's sacrifice for it, my flippant behavior causes me deep sadness. It's my prayer that when I can't hold my sons accountable, their awareness of, reverence toward, and respect for God will, and that He'll grow that in them both, the exact same way He has in me.

Revealed Sin

Unfortunately, reverence and respect were two qualities Joseph's brothers seemed to lack entirely, and that can be the case with sons of even the best parents. As I've mentioned before, it's my belief that there are no formulas for biblical parenting success, but that doesn't stop most well-meaning Christian parents from looking for them. I know amazing Christian parents who did everything "right," but their kids don't walk with the Lord. I know kids whose upbringing was anything but "Christian" in nature who love Jesus.

Jacob had the special favor of God, as did his father before him, and his father before him. God chose to birth an entire favored nation out of Jacob and his sons, and yet he was still an imperfect father who raised very imperfect children. No, we can't count on biblical formulas or righteous standing before God to produce children with hearts for the Lord, but we can count on God to reveal sin when it's time. Sometimes He does it privately, just between Him and His child. Other times, when it suits His larger purpose, He does it publicly, or maybe somewhat publicly. That's what happened with Joseph's brothers.

Many years after they sold Joseph into slavery, there was a famine in the land. By this time, Joseph had risen to a place of great importance in Egypt and had been making preparations for the famine because of a dream God had given to the pharaoh. Ironically (or maybe not), when Joseph's brothers needed food, they ended up in Egypt asking it of him. While they didn't recognize him at first, Joseph eventually revealed himself to them. When he did, they were afraid.

> Joseph said to his brothers, "I am Joseph! Is my father still living?" But they could not answer him because they were terrified in his presence.
>
> Genesis 45:3

Why were they terrified? Because their sins had finally been revealed. Not only did the brother they neglected, abused, and sold into slavery now stand before them not dead, but he was also one of the most powerful men in all the land! In addition, they would now be accountable for their actions before their father, Jacob. Who knew what Joseph would choose to do to them? Who knew how their father would respond? I'm sure all of these thoughts, and more, raced through their heads as they tried to understand what was happening to them in that overwhelming moment.

But you and I know the end of the story. Joseph embraced them and forgave them fully. He moved the entire family to be close to him in Egypt so that he could make sure they didn't go hungry, and the relationships that once seemed broken beyond repair were restored and redeemed. Acclaimed Bible teacher Warren Wiersbe wrote

> The story of Joseph and his brothers encourages us to recognize the sovereignty of God in the affairs of life and to trust His promises no matter how dark the day may be. "There are many plans in a man's heart, nevertheless the Lord's counsel—that will stand" (Proverbs 19:21, NKJV). . . . Without realizing it, Joseph's brothers were helping the Lord fulfill His covenant with Abraham.[1]

Our children are most likely going to do or say things that we don't like. They might even do evil things that bring shame on our family. We pray not, but it happens. The story of Joseph's brothers is proof that even in this situation, and no matter how long it takes, God's plan for them, the one that is for their good, to give them a future and a hope (Jeremiah 29:11) will prevail.

God's Timing

It isn't easy to trust God with our children's lives. I've often said that I would rather be in pain myself than watch my sons go through painful circumstances, but the story of Joseph and his brothers demonstrates to us that God knows what's best. He knows how to reveal our children's sin in a way that brings them to repentance, and He knows when to do it so that it brings Him the most glory and furthers His plans. Look with me at Genesis 45. At this point, twenty-two years have passed since Joseph was sold into slavery by his brothers. He's spent time in prison, and after interpreting the pharaoh's dreams revealing a coming famine, is lifted up into his service as second in command of all of Egypt. In verses 1–8, Joseph reveals his true identity to his brothers, and in verses 9–11 we find out why it all happened:

> Return quickly to my father and say to him, "This is what your son Joseph says: 'God has made me lord of all Egypt. Come down to me without delay. You can settle in the land of Goshen and be near me—you, your children, and your grandchildren, your flocks, your herds, and all you have. There I will sustain you, for there will be five more years of famine.'"

Reading the Bible from start to finish brings a little perspective: In order for God to bring the Israelites (the descendants of Jacob's family, Joseph and his brothers) up out of Egypt, sending miraculous plagues against Pharaoh and his people, parting the Red Sea, feeding them manna, and getting them to the promised land, they first had to live in Egypt. The story of Joseph and his brothers sets up the story of the Exodus. It's part of the timeline of the greater story of God.

God doesn't always show us the reason for his plans. When the time of the Exodus came, many years had passed, and "a new king, who did not know about Joseph, came to power in Egypt" (Exodus 1:8). When he was being sold as a slave by the people who were supposed to love and protect him, Joseph couldn't see God's big for-all-of-eternity plan and how it involved him and his family. And even when he did begin to see God's plan, it was still limited to how it touched his own family. He didn't know about Moses, Aaron, Joshua, or the other men to come who would lead God's people in the next steps of the journey, but he was as necessary to what we now know as Jewish history as anyone else.

Here's what I'm saying: God will make the hidden things known in the time that best suits His greater plan, and He will do it in a way that brings glory to Him. More than that, He will use the process to teach our children to revere Him. When that happens, our children have officially entered a cycle created for their good, because when they see the good hand of God and learn that He can be trusted even with their failures and flops, they'll be more inclined to trust Him the next time they have a need. Their trust and honor of Him will grow stronger and stronger as He uses them for the beautiful purpose for which they were created.

Every parent reading this sees the good news it represents, while at the same time lamenting the time it can take for God's good plans to redeem difficult circumstances. We wish for it now instead of later—now, when we can see it with our own eyes and experience the joy of our answered prayers. But that is not always how it works in God's economy. We and our sons are a blip on God's radar. An important blip, as all of God's children are, but a blip nonetheless. Even those like Abraham, Isaac, Jacob, and Joseph, who had special favor with God, had to wait at times on his perfect timing. But that doesn't mean we can't pray. God faithfully hears our prayers for our sons and will answer those prayers in His own time.

We can believe it.

"LORD, MAKE THE HIDDEN THINGS KNOWN" PRAYERS

Luke 8:17—"For nothing is concealed that won't be revealed, and nothing hidden that won't be made known and brought to light."

> **PRAYER:** Lord, make the hidden things that need to be known about _____ known, at just the right time, in a way that brings you glory. In Jesus' name, Amen.

Jeremiah 33:3—"Call to me and I will answer you and tell you great and incomprehensible things you do not know."

> **PRAYER:** Father, I am calling. Answer me and tell me what I need to know. Open my eyes to what I need to see so that I can lead _____ to you. In Jesus' name, Amen.

Galatians 6:7—"Don't be deceived: God is not mocked. For whatever a person sows he will also reap."

> **PRAYER:** Lord, teach _____ to think carefully about what he sows in this life. For what he sows he will also reap. In Jesus' name, Amen.

Psalm 139:7–12—"Where can I go to escape your Spirit? Where can I flee from your presence? If I go up to heaven, you are there; if I make my bed in Sheol, you are there. If I fly on the wings of the dawn and settle down on the western horizon, even there your hand will lead me; your right hand will hold on to me. If I say, 'Surely the darkness will hide me, and the light around me will be night'—even the darkness is not dark to you. The night shines like the day; darkness and light are alike to you."

PRAYER: Father, I take comfort in the fact that even when I can't see _____, you can. There's nowhere he can go, nothing he can do, and no place he can hide that he is outside the boundary of your love and your presence. Find him when he's in the dark and bring him into your light. In Jesus' name, Amen.

Jeremiah 29:11—"'For I know the plans I have for you'—this is the LORD's declaration—'plans for your well-being, not for disaster, to give you a future and a hope.'"

PRAYER: Lord, I believe your plans for _____ are good. Help me trust you with the timing of them. Lead him toward a future and a hope. In Jesus' name, Amen.

Philippians 1:6—"I am sure of this, that he who started a good work in you will carry it on to completion until the day of Christ Jesus."

PRAYER: Lord, finish the work you started in _____. Carry it on to completion until he is with you in heaven. In Jesus' name, Amen.

Romans 15:13—"Now may the God of hope fill you with all joy and peace as you believe so that you may overflow with hope by the power of the Holy Spirit."

PRAYER: Father, you are the God of hope. Fill _____ with all joy and peace as he believes so that he may overflow with hope by the power of your Holy Spirit. In Jesus' name, Amen.

Proverbs 19:20–21—"Listen to counsel and receive instruction so that you may be wise later in life. Many plans are in a person's heart, but the LORD's decree will prevail."

PRAYER: Lord, help _____ listen to counsel and receive instruction so that he can be wise for all of his days. May your plans for his life prevail over his. In Jesus' name, Amen.

Proverbs 3:5–6—"Trust in the LORD with all your heart, and do not rely on your own understanding; in all your ways know him, and he will make your paths straight."

PRAYER: Father, help _____ to trust you with all his heart and not rely on his own understanding. In all of his ways, may he know you. Make his paths straight. In Jesus' name, Amen.

Second Corinthians 4:17–18—"For our momentary light affliction is producing for us an absolutely incomparable eternal weight of glory. So we do not focus on what is seen, but on what is unseen. For what is seen is temporary, but what is unseen is eternal."

PRAYER: Lord, help _____ not to get caught up in what he can see, but instead to focus on what is unseen. Help him to have an eternal perspective today, and for the rest of his life. In Jesus' name, Amen.

PRAYERS AND NOTES

ACKNOWLEDGMENTS

Cory: You're my buffer, my backbone, my protector, and my friend. You serve me so well and have consistently given our boys an excellent example of what it means to love a wife and family well. I love you!

Max and Sam: This book is a work of my heart, and that's because the two of you have been the primary work of my heart for almost twenty years. You've pushed me in so many ways, sometimes so hard that all my ugly came out, but I'm grateful to have had the opportunity to see my heart so that I could offer it to Jesus to fix. No matter what, loving you has pushed me to be the very best version of myself that I can, because I wanted the opportunity to show you what it looks like to love others with everything you have. I wanted to teach you to run to Jesus. I wanted to create a world that pointed you to Him and teach you to see the world the way He does. If I've gotten any of that right, all credit goes to Him. Most of all, you have pushed me to be a praying mom, because I know that if God doesn't show up and work in spite of me, nothing happens. You're my absolute favorites, and I will never stop fighting for your good, and God's best.

Mom and Dad: You sacrificed, and gave, and gave, and sacrificed some more so that I could follow my dreams and live out my purpose. And you've done the same thing for the boys. You're a wonderful example of what it means to take care of your family. None of this would've been possible without you.

I dedicated *Praying for Boys* to my grandmothers, Catherine Trout Lloyd (Cack) and Wanda Jewel McDonald (Duel). Both of them, in their own ways, influenced me to be who I am today, so I'd like to mention them again here. Cack taught me by example what it looks like to fight for your family and refuse to give up. Duel taught me how to make amazing chicken casserole and, perhaps more importantly, showed me the value of prayer. These two concepts laid the groundwork for the way I've chosen to parent my boys and will hopefully influence generations to come. I'm so grateful for them both and look forward to seeing them again in glory.

Jeff Braun: Thank you for believing in this work. You've always seen the vision and been one of its greatest champions. I have felt the support when I needed it most.

Chip MacGregor: This is the last book we'll work on together, and it's been a wonderful ride. You helped me bring the first *Praying for Boys* into the world, and it's fitting that *Praying for Teen Boys* should be our last project as you retire. Thank you for all the ways you've gone over and above for me for over a decade. There are a handful of things I might not have survived had it not been for your counsel, and I'm eternally grateful for your wisdom and support.

Ellen McAuley: Thank you for your insightful edits on the book. I've never written anything that wasn't made better by a good editor, and you were exactly that.

The Million Praying Moms family (previously the MOB Society family): I'm not even sure where to start. You have been so precious to me. I've spent over a decade of my life thinking about you, praying for you, and asking God what to share with you that would make a difference in your life for the sake of the gospel. To me, the investment has had generational implications. My desire has been not only to reach your heart with the message that prayer is not a last resort, but to change the dynamic of your home as you pray, knowing that if you are the only variable that changes, the entire outcome changes. My bold, audacious prayer has been that entire family lines would be changed for the sake of the kingdom because of these ministries. Thank you for the opportunity to speak to you like we're sitting across from each other in a coffee shop for all these years.

Stacey Thacker: I'm happy to be stuck with you.

Jesus: Thank you.

NOTES

The Power of Fighting FOR Instead of Against

1. Timothy Keller, *Prayer: Experiencing Awe and Intimacy with God* (New York: Dutton, 2014), 48.
2. Brooke McGlothlin, *Praying Mom* (Minneapolis: Bethany House, 2021), 45–47.
3. Brooke McGlothlin, *Praying for Boys: Asking God for the Things They Need Most* (Minneapolis: Bethany House, 2014), 52–54.

Chapter 1 Lord, Show Me

1. Adapted from Brooke McGlothlin, *Praying for Boys*, 21.
2. E. M. Bounds, "The Purpose of Prayer" in *The Classic Collection on Prayer* (New Kensington, PA: Bridge Logos, 2002), 510.
3. George Muller, *The Autobiography of George Muller* (Springdale, PA: Whitaker House, 1984), 132.

Chapter 3 Lord, Keep His Heart

1. Crossway Bibles. *The ESV Study Bible: English Standard Version* (Wheaton, IL: Crossway Bibles, 2008), 1142.
2. *Matthew Henry Commentary on the Whole Bible (Complete)*, www.biblestudytools.com/commentaries/matthew-henry-complete/proverbs/4.html.
3. Tony Evans, "Encountering the Power of God," November 18, 2020, www.youtube.com/watch?v=RzhuOHrhXeQ.
4. Brooke McGlothlin, *Everyday Prayers for Peace* (New Kensington, PA: Whitaker House, 2022), 64.
5. Preston Perry and Jackie Hill Perry, "Guarding Your Heart in Marriage," With the Perrys, July 14, 2022, www.youtube.com/watch?v=9AJCu5qE04I.

Chapter 4 Lord, Let Him Hear Wisdom

1. Tony Evans, *Tony Evans Bible Commentary* (Nashville, TN: Holman Bible Publishers, 2019), 499.
2. Skip Heitzig, "A Superhero Loses His Cape," Calvary Church with Skip Heitzig, November 7, 2016, www.youtube.com/watch?v=qPCp6MQYGBw.

3. Warren W. Wiersbe, *The Wiersbe Bible Commentary: Old Testament* (Colorado Springs: David C. Cook, 2007), 459.

Chapter 5 Lord, Place a Guard Over His Mouth

1. Ward Harris, phone call conversation, November 16, 2023.

2. Lucy Debenham, "Communication—What Percentage Is Body Language?" Body Language Expert, September 13, 2020, www.bodylanguage-expert.co.uk/communication-what-percentage-body-language.html.

3. Warren W. Wiersbe, *The Wiersbe Bible Commentary: New Testament* (Colorado Springs: David C. Cook, 2007), 202.

Chapter 6 Lord, Help Him Stand

1. *The Tony Evans Bible Commentary*, 506.

2. Matthew Henry Commentary on the Whole Bible (Complete), www.biblestudytools.com/commentaries/matthew-henry-complete/colossians/2.html.

3. Brooke McGlothlin, *Everyday Prayers for Patience* (New Kensington, PA: Whitaker House, 2023), 100–101.

4. Matthew Henry Commentary on the Whole Bible (Complete), www.biblestudytools.com/commentaries/matthew-henry-complete/1-peter/5.html.

5. Matthew Henry Commentary on the Whole Bible (Complete), www.biblestudytools.com/commentaries/matthew-henry-complete/1-peter/5.html.

6. George Morrison, *Morrison on James through Revelation* (Chattanooga, TN: AMG, 1984), 34, quoted in "How Do Followers of Jesus Handle Our Anxiety?" Jesus Quotes and God Thoughts, October 7, 2020, https://quotesthoughtsrandom.wordpress.com/2020/10/07/17793.

Chapter 7 Lord, Open His Eyes

1. R. C. Sproul, *St. Andrew's Expositional Commentary*, *Romans* (Wheaton: Crossway, 2009), 39.

Chapter 8 Lord, Give Him a Heart After You

1. Billy Graham, "If God is perfect, why does He get angry? Isn't that a sin?" Billy Graham Evangelistic Association, December 10, 2021, https://billygraham.org/answer/how-is-gods-anger-different-than-mans-anger./

2. Erin H. Warren, *Everyday Prayers for Faith: Finding Confidence in God No Matter What* (New Kensington, PA: Whitaker House, 2024), 11.

3. Erin H. Warren, "How to Keep the Faith in Your Hard Stories," Interview with Erin H. Warren and Michele Cushatt, Million Praying Moms Instagram, www.instagram.com/reel/C2NVqkxr2LJ.

4. Amanda Williams, "The 7000 Promises of God: An In-Depth Look" Christian Website, www.christianwebsite.com/what-are-the-7000-promises-of-god.

5. Brooke McGlothlin, *Praying for Boys*, 102–103.

Chapter 9 Lord, Make the Hidden Things Known

1. *The Wiersbe Bible Commentary: Old Testament*, 131.

BROOKE MCGLOTHLIN has encouraged thousands of moms toward a richer prayer life for over a decade. She is the founder of Million Praying Moms and host of the *Everyday Prayers with Million Praying Moms* podcast, a popular online ministry that exists to help moms make prayer their first and best response to the challenges of parenting. Brooke is the author of several books and resources for moms and lives in the mountains of southwest Virginia with her husband and their two sons.

CONNECT WITH BROOKE MCGLOTHLIN

MillionPrayingMoms.com

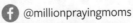 @millionprayingmoms

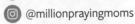 @millionprayingmoms

You May Also Like . . .

Helping you navigate the complicated teen years—and your changing relationship—with your daughter, Stacey Thacker offers wisdom, practical help, and over 90 Scripture-inspired prayers to help you fight *for* your teen, not *against* her. Feel purposeful, not powerless, in your parenting as you partner with God in prayer— and rediscover the joy of being her mom.

Praying for Teen Girls

PRAYERS AND NOTES

PRAYERS AND NOTES

PRAYERS AND NOTES

PRAYERS AND NOTES

PRAYERS AND NOTES

PRAYERS AND NOTES

PRAYERS AND NOTES

PRAYERS AND NOTES

PRAYERS AND NOTES

PRAYERS AND NOTES

PRAYERS AND NOTES